DATE

14 DAY LOAN

UNCIVILIZED BEASTS

and

SHAMELESS HELLIONS

UNCIVILIZED BEASTS

and

SHAMELESS HELLIONS

TRAVELS WITH AN
NPR CORRESPONDENT

JOHN F. BURNETT

Rodale books may be purchased for business or promotional use or for special sales.
For information, please write to:
Special Markets Department, Rodale Inc., 733 Third Avenue, New York, NY 10017

Printed in the United States of America

Rodale Inc. makes every effort to use acid-free ⊗, recycled paper ♻.

Book design by Christopher Rhoads

Library of Congress Cataloging-in-Publication Data

Burnett, John F.
  Uncivilized beasts and shameless hellions : travels with an NPR correspondent /
John F. Burnett.
    p.   cm.
  ISBN-13 978-1-59486-304-2   hardcover
  ISBN-10 1-59486-304-0   hardcover
  1. Burnett, John F.   2. Radio journalists—United States—Biography.   I. Title.
PN4874.B843A3   2006
070.92—dc22
[B]   2006018443

Distributed to the trade by Holtzbrinck Publishers

2   4   6   8   10   9   7   5   3   1   hardcover

We inspire and enable people to improve their lives and the world around them
For more of our products visit rodalestore.com or call 800-848-4735

For Ginny, my twin flame

"Everything is superb and breathtaking.
I am crawling forward on my belly like they do in the movies."

—DIANE ARBUS

CONTENTS

ACKNOWLEDGMENTS

TO MY WIFE, GINNY, for everything; to my children, Willie, Grant, and Helen, for putting up with my absences; to my sister, Elizabeth, for her companionship, her editing skills, and her suggestion a long time ago that I switch from psychology to journalism; to Mama, for her unconditional love and steadfast support over the years; and to Papa, for passing on to me his love of words, music, and thunderstorms. To my high school English teacher, Christine Eastus, who urged me to write; and to my first newspaper editor, Sue Watkins, who embodies the values and integrity of the best of this business.

To all the editors at National Public Radio whose skill and friendship have guided me for 20 years: Barbara Rehm, Anthony Brooks, Anne Edwards, Cindy Johnston, Michael Fields, Larry Abramson, Pat Flynn, Chris Joyce, Marc Rosenbaum, Cathy Shaw, Alisa Barba, Janet Domowitz, Tom Cole, Doug Roberts, Ted Clark, Didi Schanche, and Loren Jenkins, but especially Bebe Crouse and Ellen Weiss. To the king of the intercontinental fixers, Bob Duncan. To Will Van Overbeek, for his assistance with the photographs. To Jennifer Pearl and Andi Sporkin, for their enthusiastic help in promoting the book. And to Clifford Richardson, for building El Ranchito de La Virginia in Abiquiu.

To my friends who offered me support and encouragement during these past two years: Bill Crawford, Ricardo Ainslie, Larry Wright, Bill Minutaglio, Turk Pipkin, Davia Nelson, Stewart Vanderwilt, and Peter Breslow; to those who provided help on individual chapters: Guillermo H. Cantú, Larry Fitzgerald, Dita Dauti, Anne Hawke, Wade Goodwyn, Katie Smith Milway, Milton Flores-Barahona, Jim Magnuson, and Los Aficionados de Los Angeles; to my agent, James Levine; to my editor, Zachary Schisgal, at Rodale Press; to Cynthia Hughes Literary Services and fact-checker Amy Tharp Nylund; and to my colleague Dave McNeely, who was the first to say, "Hey, you oughta write a book."

INTRODUCTION

T ALL BEGAN in Guatemala. In 1983, I quit my job at the *San Antonio Express-News* and moved to Central America to learn Spanish and try to be a foreign correspondent. Guatemala was in the midst of a savage civil war that was largely overlooked by the US media. And so for two years, I worked in Guatemala City as a stringer for United Press International, learning about life, death, love, and corruption.

Jeep Wagoneers with tinted windows raced through darkened streets on awful errands that yielded roadside corpses in the mornings. No one wanted to acknowledge the violence because they were too terrified that the secret police would construe their outrage as dissent. Then they too would end up as one of the *muertecitos*—the little deaths—announced daily in *Prensa Libre*, the *Free Press*, which, of course, wasn't free at all.

Then came radio. One afternoon, I attended a religious revival in a soccer stadium in Guatemala City where Maya Indians in the audience began to speak in tongues as the service climaxed. I walked along the bleachers, holding out a cheap Radio Shack stereo microphone plugged into a Sony Walkman. Later that day, I slipped on a pair of headphones, pushed "PLAY," and had my "aha" moment. Into my ears came the sound of mystical, ecstatic voices rising and falling in cadence with the spirit. I was hypnotized. I was hooked. No print story could convey that sound. Within a month, I filed my first radio story for an independent program called Latin American News Service. "Write shorter sentences and record lots of ambience," the editor, Maria

Martin, told me. Now in my twentieth year with National Public Radio, I'm still hooked.

Radio is cool. There's something that happens when voice and natural sound come together to transport listeners out of their surroundings. It only happens with radio. NPR calls it "the driveway moment"—when people sit in the car to wait until the story is over. Garrison Keillor calls it "the theater of the mind." But even at NPR there's only so much you can squeeze into a 7½-minute story.

After deadline, reporters don't talk about the who, what, where, why, and when. We talk about the sixth W, the *whoa*—bizarre encounters, miserable journeys, horrible hotels, great fixers, dangerous highways, gruesome dead people, gruesome live people, and unsung heroes. This book is my attempt to make sense of it all, to sort through the beasts and the hellions.

What follow are reflections on 11 stories and people that I have covered. But they're not just story subjects. They have become part of me. These are the voices that haunted me long after the reports aired: the marine artillery sergeant, the Pakistani fixer, the Maya widow, the death chamber chaplain, the Mexican street musician, the bullfighter, the Katrina survivor. Most of them aired on NPR.

When I joined NPR in 1986, we were essentially a supplemental news source. Though we covered the news of the day, we were best known for the breath-by-breath account of a trek up Everest or long treatises on maple sugaring, hammer dulcimers, and clown colleges. In those days I often had to explain to people who we were. "It's the *radio* side of PBS. Think of the BBC for America." One night I was at a Fort Worth rodeo arena recording a bull rider when the announcer drawled over the PA system, "We want to welcome National Public Rodeo." The cowboy crowd, in hats and boots, whooped in delight, believing Washington had finally funded something they cared about.

People don't confuse us anymore. In 1981, we had 270 noncommercial stations and a weekly audience of about seven million. Twenty-five years later, the number of member stations has tripled to more than 800, and our audience has catapulted to more than 25 million listeners a week. We have the second and third most listened-to programs on the radio. We maintain news bureaus in 37 cities, domestic and worldwide, staffed with correspondents whom I'm honored to call my colleagues. Today, people still expect us to do the *Radio Expeditions* on tiger hunters in Nepal but also to be on the scene and on the air when regimes tumble and wars break out.

For me, journalism ceased being a job long ago. It's an addiction. I travel and feast, take notes and move on, awestruck and insatiable. I tell journalism students what my father told me, somewhat enviously, as he sat behind the desk of his small advertising agency in Dallas: "Reporters have a skeleton key to the world."

We also have a terribly important responsibility. Pete Hamill wrote, "The reporter is the member of the tribe who is sent to the back of the cave to find out what's there." That's why it's so frustrating that we keep tripping over ourselves. The press has metamorphosed from a corps—connoting a sense of order and belonging—into what many people see as a giant octopus: massive, fleshy, many tentacled, and befogged in its own ink. It strikes me that oftentimes the more of us there are, the more likely we are to get it wrong. That's in this book, too. Add to that an army of public affairs people and spin doctors who have elevated media manipulation to new heights. There has never been a more critical time for us to take our torches—and microphones—deep into the cave.

SECTION I

CALAMITIES

Chapter 1

KATRINA:
THE BIG ONE

THE MISSISSIPPI RIVER has begun to flow backward. White-caps on the river are breaking upstream. The Father of Waters is in reverse. It's a titanic contest of natural forces fought between the cumulative drainage of 1.5 million square miles of continent and a mammoth storm surge from the gulf. The hurricane is winning.

Down on the Poydras Street wharf, all that's left of an American flag is a field of stars. Wind peels stucco from the side of a shopping mall and flings it into the sky. Palm trees flail like wild mop tops.

Suddenly, a 160-foot-long dry dock, the *Miss Darby*, tears loose from its mooring across the river on Algiers Point and sails upriver like a leaf on a pond. The errant seacraft, girdling a red tugboat, narrowly misses a stanchion under the huge cantilevered bridge called the Crescent City Connection, then continues upstream for another mile and plows into a small tanker docked at the Stone Energy Fuel Terminal on the West Bank. The dry dock tears a 13-foot gash in the ship from which gushes 56,141 gallons of diesel, lurches past, and finally slams into the earthen levee at the foot of Lafayette Street in Gretna, causing the police chief to fear the mighty river will roar into his city at any moment. Under normal circumstances, the flight of the *Miss Darby* would warrant a story on the front of the Metro section of the *Times-Picayune*, but it's a mere sideshow to the epic that is to be Hurricane Katrina. The storm will be the nation's worst natural disaster in modern history and for me the culminating horror of 26 years in journalism.

It's dawn on August 29, 2005. The NPR Katrina crew—correspondent Greg Allen, producers Muthoni Muturi and Anne Hawke, and me—are hunkered down in the Hilton Riverside Hotel. This is a good place to be. The ¾-inch-thick glass in the hotel windows is rated to withstand 150-mph winds, and the view is spectacular. The morning sky is a milky blue haze, as if opening my eyes underwater. We've heard the howling wind since 3:00 a.m. and felt the high-rise sway in the dark like a treehouse. Now we can finally witness the great cyclone's arrival.

"The hotel we're in is swaying and creaking like an old ship at sea, and the water in the bathtub is sloshing back and forth. Katrina has arrived," I tell Renée Montagne, the *Morning Edition* cohost.

By 7:00 a.m., the storm's eye is driving north along a line about 15 miles east of New Orleans, heading for the mouth of the Pearl River. This is good news for us. It puts the most dangerous quadrant of the rotating hurricane to the northeast of the city, but it means residents on the Mississippi Gulf Coast need to hurry and get right with the Lord. A relieved public official speaking on New Orleans radio station WWL—which will broadcast heroically throughout the crisis—says it is "the best of a worst-case scenario."

I used to love covering hurricanes...until Katrina. Hurricanes are the crystal meth of journalism. There's nothing like racing toward a big storm on a deserted highway while the opposite lanes are gridlocked with people trying to get out. You never know exactly where it's going to hit, but you try to position yourself as close to landfall as possible without being in the eye. You want to be where the action is. Local TV reporters in sporty rainsuits who've been caterwauling for days about the approaching storm are secretly disappointed if it smashes some market other than their own.

At this point, Hurricane Katrina feels like a half-dozen other hurricanes I've covered up and down the Gulf Coast and Atlantic seaboard. In my mind's ear, I'm predicting the interviews I'll get in the coming days: wisecracking residents who rode it out, relieved returnees, sweating utility crews, laconic cops. I'm already thinking about the Cajun sausage I'll pick up on the drive back to Austin in a couple of days.

How wrong I'll be.

At this early stage, no one has any idea that within 48 hours, an inundated city will descend into chaos, more than 1,100 souls will perish, and the tragedy will be deepened by a response from a confederacy of dunces.

Conditions are worsening across the city. The real-time, on-line storm blog of the *Times-Picayune* has unconfirmed reports of a levee breach on the Industrial Canal, severe flooding in Arabi and the Lower Ninth Ward, the twin Interstate-10 bridges destroyed, and the giant root-beer mug at the Frost Top toppled onto its creamy head. But power is out throughout the city, so nobody in New Orleans can read what's happening. Information on WWL is sketchy. They're saying New Orleans "dodged the bullet."

By midafternoon, the last cottony bands of the storm lumber north under an angry gray sky. I'm getting stir-crazy. It's time to start reporting. I venture down the darkened stairwell, past clusters of anxious guests. They've had a terrifying morning. The wind tore off sections of aluminum roofing, and rain poured onto 600 Hilton employees and their families camped out on the indoor tennis courts. Then the gale snatched up a snack-bar cabana in the third-floor pool area and hurled it through plate glass, sending more panicked guests fleeing to lower floors.

I step out of the side service doors, and it feels good to escape the suffocating building. The air outside is muggy and blustery. The ground is littered with broken glass and hundreds of twisted aluminum awning strips that rattle like snakes with every gust.

Allen returns from a walk to the French Quarter. "Be careful," he says. "I just had a shop owner pull a pistol on me. People are freaked out."

It's a luxury to have two reporters on a big story—one files for *All Things Considered* while the other takes *Morning Edition*. The national desk gives me *Morning,* which is great because I have more time to file, but it also means I'll have to work in the dark.

Muturi and I walk to the Vieux Carre to look around. The Quarter is mostly high and dry. The doors have blown off the Daiquiri Deli. Behind St. Louis Cathedral, a massive live oak and a magnolia have crashed to the ground around a statue of Jesus, unscathed but for a broken thumb. Good Catholics will consider it a divine act.

The city is in agony, but we don't know it yet. We can't venture far, reports of flooding are unconfirmed, and it's getting dark. We walk the eight blocks back to the Hilton to put the story together. Standing at the window in my room, I can barely make out the great river as it flows through the darkened metropolis because there are no lights reflecting on the water. I open my laptop, switch on my headlamp, reach for a Clif Bar, and start writing. Muturi, a Kenyan journalist who came to NPR as a grad student from American University, logs tape. The hotel room is sealed as tight as a tomb, and sweat runs down my back.

At midnight, we're ready to file. Hawke has set up the satellite phone on the roof of the parking garage next door, but to get there requires a labyrinthine journey through the unlit hotel complex. We descent 21 flights of stairs and walk past the employee cafeteria, go across piles of soaked bath towels that squish underfoot like spring tundra, pass the giant Louis Armstrong statue, exit the side door, cross the parking lot, climb eight flights of stairs, and finally emerge—20 minutes later—on the top level of the garage. There, between rain puddles and broken glass, the sat phone blinks alive, and the voice of a crabby overnight engineer in Washington comes over the headphones.

"It's really loud where you are."

"I know that. It's a generator."

"Can you move farther away from that thing?"

"No, this is the only place we could find to hit the satellite."

"Can you put something over your head to muffle the sound?"

Hawke gets a rain slicker and throws it over my head, and I read a few more lines.

The engineer sighs audibly. "That's a little better," she says. "Go ahead, I'm rolling."

Even as I'm reading the story, I know it's incomplete. All I've seen is the French Quarter, but it's all I've got at the moment. Reporting can be frustrating like that. The same thing happened on the road to Iraq. All we knew was what our marine unit saw. Journalism through a periscope.

I fall into bed at 1:00 a.m. in our airless room and sleep dreamlessly.

She started on August 23 over the southeastern Bahamas as Tropical Depression Number 12. Two days later, she'd barely earned her name, Katrina, when she blew across Miami-Dade and Broward Counties, Florida, with 80 mph winds. Her punch was surprisingly strong for a Category 1. Nine people died, and more than a million lost power.

When Katrina plunged into the Gulf of Mexico, climatologists recognized that oceanic and atmospheric conditions were ideal for the creation of a superstorm. Surface sea temperatures were two or three degrees higher than usual—in fact, it was the warmest gulf in 115 years. Like a heat-seeking missile, Katrina found the Loop Current, whose tepid waters extend down 200 feet. Moist, warm air raced upward into her vortex, revving her convective engine faster and faster. Forty thousand feet up in the troposphere, a large upper-level anticyclone was positioned to act like an exhaust fan and carry away her ferocious winds, thus reducing the wind shear that normally tears apart the internal structure of a big hurricane. She was rapidly strengthening, every 20 minutes releasing an amount of energy equivalent to the explosion of a 10-megaton nuclear bomb. Katrina was invincible.

On the Sunday before landfall, Katrina exploded with 175-mph winds, into a Category 5, the highest category on the Saffir-Simpson Hurricane Scale. Her wind field had doubled in size, filling the entire gulf with rain bands that simultaneously touched Merida, Mexico; Havana, Cuba; Naples, Florida; and Grande Isle, Louisiana.

The final act commenced when a midlevel low-pressure system over Texas retreated westward, which steered the massive storm on a north-northwesterly course toward Louisiana. Anyone watching could see what was happening. She had turned. She was coming to New Orleans, the lowest-lying city in America. The Big One had arrived.

At around 5:30 a.m. Monday, Katrina made her first landfall at Plaquemines Parish, the toe on the boot of Louisiana, the traditional province of oystermen, shrimpers, and political bosses. With the deterioration of her inner eyewall, she had diminished to a high Category

3 with sustained top winds of 127 mph. According to the authoritative *Tropical Cyclone Report* written by the National Hurricane Center, Katrina's winds were never that fearsome; it was her tidal surge. Twenty-four hours earlier, when she was still a Cat 5 out in the gulf, she generated an immense surge tide of northward swells that never ebbed. At 5:00 a.m. the morning the storm struck, buoy 42040, located 74 miles south of Dauphin Island, Alabama, reported a wave 55 feet tall—the highest ever measured by the National Data Buoy Center. When the great mound of water reached the coast, the Mississippi Emergency Operations Center in Hancock County observed an unofficial tide height of 28 feet.

In the fishing town of Empire, Plaquemines Parish, wind and water lifted St. Ann Catholic Church off its foundation, spun it 1¼ turns, jammed a magnolia tree into the narthex, and submerged a plaster statue of Jesus up to his sacred heart. That was just the warmup act.

I awake on Tuesday to the news that the city is a water world.

Mayor C. Ray Nagin Jr., the 49-year-old former cable TV executive and city hall reformer, is announcing on WWL that 80 percent of his city is under water. Levees have ruptured along the lake, and the mayor says people are stranded on rooftops throughout the Lower Ninth Ward, New Orleans East, and St. Bernard Parish. "We are calling on anyone with a boat to come and help rescue survivors in our city," Nagin says in an urgent voice.

Most of downtown and the adjacent French Quarter are unflooded because they're situated on the ancient alluvial deposits along the Mississippi, which are higher than the rest of the below-sea-level city. Running on adrenaline and peanut butter, I scramble into the cab of my rented Ford F-150 with Hawke. Praying I don't puncture a tire, I gingerly drive over a carpet of broken glass and pull out of the parking garage and onto the streets of the drowned city.

Progress is slow. We keep doubling back after encountering underwater streets and fallen oaks, their branches festooned with muddy Mardi Gras beads. At a corner newspaper stand, the last edition of the *Times-Picayune* screams, "Katrina Takes Aim."

The city has taken a frightful beating. I feel a deep sadness, as though a beloved queen has died. I've been coming to New Orleans ever since 1969, when my father took me to Preservation Hall to hear the aging jazz pianist Sweet Emma and let me peek at the nudie dancers on Bourbon Street. Later, in 1983, I flew into town to romance my future wife, Ginny Garrard, a graduate student at Tulane University. We spent long, dissolute weekends in the moldering former slave quarters where she lived on Burdette Street and explored the hidden delights of Uptown: boiled crawfish at Frankie and Johnny's, mint-chocolate ice at Plum Street Sno-Balls, pecan waffles at the Camelia Grill. The day she received her PhD, I rented a St. Charles Avenue streetcar; and we clattered down the tracks between Brahmin mansions, drinking champagne and listening to Brazilian music. This was a city in which to fall in love.

After joining NPR in 1986, I leaped at any chance to travel to the Big Easy. With every visit, I succumbed further to the charms of this voluptuous and indolent city. It was the warm spring afternoon in 2000 I spent cruising the old neighborhoods with piano professor Dr. John, aka Mac Rebennack, that I felt I finally glimpsed the city's soul. In his thick New Orleans brogue, Rebennack told me, "Any po' community—and N'awlins is basically a po' community—the po'ness is replaced by richness in the art of the music, the food, all of the things that is of the spirit. Nobody plans stuff to be that way. It's just a thing that happens." During a tour of the devastated Ninth Ward months after the storm, a visibly shaken Rebennack told me his beloved city had been "traumaticalized."

On the morning after Katrina, there's no time for sentimentality. Like maritime explorers, we must discover a way through this watery realm. Finally, we find a route past the old US Mint, up Elysian Fields to St. Claude Avenue, where we creep past dingy bars and beauty salons in water up to the hubcaps. At Music Street, the water reaches the bumper; and I park the truck on the neutral ground, the only dry spot on the avenue. Then we see them.

People are coming from all directions out of the pooled neighborhoods, like wraiths returning from a drowning. Water stretches as far as the eye can see and has a strangely quieting effect, as if we've come upon an urban oasis. The usual city din of bus and auto and siren is gone; there is no sound save the splashing of feet and the occasional shout of distress or recognition or drunkenness.

James Ackerson Jr., 56, stands in the still-clear water in a filthy T-shirt and dark trousers, unshaven and hollow-eyed. He's a carpenter at Charity Hospital and lives in the Lower Ninth Ward near the historic Jackson Barracks, one of the lowest spots in the city.

"It's devastatin', bad, terrible," he says, struggling to find words and hold his composure. "They got people drownin' back there. My son and a friend of his come up in a boat and just got me. I was on the roof for 24 hours, and water had to be 12 feet high. Farther back to Florida Avenue it's 15 to 18 feet high." He wipes tears from his eyes. "There's still people on rooftops, elderly people, children, women. They need help back there. Please help 'em," Ackerman pleads. I experience the first wave of uselessness that will return again and again all week. Without a rescue boat, food, water, or helpful information, all we can do is take testimonies and promise to get the word out.

A bedraggled family with 10 children in tow comes up the street, pulling a bright orange swim float. The mother, Denise Williams, who is barefoot, spots our microphone. "Can y'all find any help for us? Please, we don't have anywhere to go," she says. "We're just walkin' with all these kids with nothin' to eat."

Her husband, Louis, a big man with a deep voice, breaks in: "Somebody needs to go over there and get them three old womens in wheelchairs. They're in the school. We done give 'em all the food and water we had. We couldn't take 'em with us."

At this moment, the refugees are realizing the same thing we are: Everything is gone—electricity, drinking water, sanitation, 911 service, traversable streets, grocery stores, emergency rooms, drive-thru daiquiri stands. It's all gone. No American city in modern times has faced this kind of catastrophe. When terrorists flew jets into the Twin Towers, at least New York City's infrastructure remained intact to allow for an orderly rescue and recovery. In contrast, New Orleans is dissolving in the floodwaters. It has become, in the words of one stranded evacuee, medieval.

A few blocks down St. Claude, a boisterous crowd outside Roberts Market Fare decides it's time, as they say in New Orleans, "for makin' groceries." I park the truck on the neutral ground, and we slosh through ankle-deep water to the storefront, being careful not to stumble on the submerged curb. They've pried open the metal shutter protecting the entrance to the supermarket. Men and women, old and young, and a few kids are streaming out of the doorway. Some clutch half-gallons of liquor. Others push shopping carts laden with food, cigarettes, makeup, disposable diapers, and booze. The atmosphere is festive but wary. A few pull their shirts over their faces when they see us.

The scene is semisurvival, semicriminal, and I'm at a loss as to what to ask the shopper/looters. A well-groomed, middle-aged woman is leaning on a cart full of fruit, candy, and bread. Hawke holds out the microphone and says cheerfully, "Looks like you've got some good stuff."

"We ain't got nuttin'. We only got the clothes on our backs," answers the woman, who gives her name as Muriel. "We walked from the Lower Ninth Ward. I'm sorry, but I ain't never been like this in my life. I always worked for myself. I ain't never thought I'd have to do this." She looks at her purloined groceries and begins to weep. "We got in the attic and the water started risin'. And the water kept risin', so we had to get outta there. And we walked along the electric wires to the top of another house that was higher than ours. And all that wind! My old man went down twice, and I called his name and he came back up. There is a God."

While she's talking, a man in a Saints T-shirt is hauling great armfuls of snacks and liquor toward the open trunk of an SUV parked next to my truck. He yells to the driver, "C'mere, man, we takin' *alla* this shit. C'mon, man, pack this motherfucker *up*."

Muriel watches him dolefully. "I hope we don't go to jail 'cause we don't have anything to eat," she says. "And I been hungry for two days. I am so sorry to be goin' through this."

As we're leaving, a New Orleans Police Department (NOPD) squad car, the first we've seen all morning, drives slowly past the free-for-all without stopping. We follow. When it turns into the French Quarter, I flag down the vehicle, walk over, and ask the female officer, "Why don't you try to stop the looting?"

She looks hard at my face, then says with annoyance, "I don't have time for this," and drives away.

We want to explore the city, but the only area that's drivable is a narrow crescent of land that hugs the Mississippi and extends out about three-quarters of a mile. The rest is lake. Hawke and I thread our way through the Quarter and cross Canal Street—now a wasteland of toppled palm trees—and stop at the water's edge at Loyola Drive. We need to see what's happening inside the Superdome, but it sits three blocks away, surrounded by water. At six-foot-seven, I cavalierly suggest we wade to the Dome. Hawke is five foot four and a half, a former media lawyer who switched to journalism because she thought it would be more fun. She may be having second thoughts on this morning.

"I so don't want to get wet," she says, handing me the equipment bag. We walk into waist-deep water reeking of the gasoline that's seeping out of swamped cars. We walk slowly and carefully so as not to trip on underwater debris. Someone has chained two Rottweilers to the front doors of Whitney Bank as an antilooting tactic, and they bark savagely at the evacuees splashing past.

We finally reach the concrete ramp to the Dome and brace ourselves for what's to come. WWL has been reporting grim conditions inside—overcrowding, sweltering heat, backed-up bathrooms, drug dealing, sexual assaults. I'm reminded of the story around town that the Superdome always brings bad luck because it was built over the Girod Street Cemetery. Uniformed national guardsmen are refusing to let people leave. They see our media credentials and open the glass doors to let us in.

It feels like an internment camp. The corridors smell of sweat, urine, and old Meals Ready to Eat. Everyone has claimed a personal space on the floor, gamely trying to defend it and stay comfortable. A large family lounges in the area between a nachos stand and a Dove Bar kiosk. When I ask how they're doing, Angela Parkman, a 37-year-old nursing student, says in a measured tone, "Everybody's under a whole lot of pressure and stress right now. They're feeding us every two hours, but it's just so hot, and they're piling more and more in."

A guardsman lets us out of the Dome with the warning to "be careful out there."

We walk back out onto the ramp and meet CNN correspondent Jeanne Meserve and producer Jim Spellman, both of whom look frazzled. We ask them how they're doing. "We've been better. How about you guys?" she says.

Reporters are living their own storm odysseys by this time. Meserve describes how they're keeping their vehicle rolling with cans of Fix-A-Flat, but they can't use their other SUVs because they're stuck in the hotel parking garage, which is surrounded by water. So they've been taking batteries out of the stranded vehicles and running them up to their hotel room to charge their equipment. "You ever run up 10 flights of stairs with a car battery?" she says, laughing.

We wade back into the rainbow-sheened water and leave the last trace of uniformed law-and-order behind at the Dome. The rest of the city is on its own. All day we drive the abandoned streets—on sidewalks, through dead streetlights, the wrong way on one-way streets—without another glimpse of police or the National Guard.

Katrina is the catastrophe the authorities imagined but never expected. New Orleans conducted annual hurricane training exercises that followed the *Comprehensive Emergency Management Plan*, a dense, acronym-filled document that spells out "the speedy yet orderly recovery of the community." Organized in phases, concepts, and tasks, the plan calls for, among other things, a mobile command center, a damage assessment officer, and a disaster relief center. None of these materialize in the chaotic days after the storm. The plan does not anticipate the mayor—without command post or communication—dashing up 23 flights of stairs in the Hyatt to get away from a mob of furious evacuees pounding on the doors in the watery streets below, according to city councilwoman Jacquelyn Clarkson, who was present.

Nagin and Louisiana governor Kathleen Babineaux Blanco are staggered by the scale of the flood and inexperienced in disasters. In her first conversation with President Bush, the governor tells him simply, "I need everything you've got," without specifying what.

On Tuesday in Washington, Michael D. Brown, head of the Federal Emergency Management Agency (FEMA), says, "Considering the dire circumstances that we have in New Orleans, virtually a city that has been destroyed, things are going relatively well."

The only FEMA on-site coordinator in New Orleans is Marty Bahamonde, a 12-year veteran of past disasters. He later concludes, "There was a systematic failure at all levels of government to understand the magnitude of the situation."

New Orleans has had water at the center of its consciousness from its beginning. The city seal bears the image of a bearded Neptune. Behind 350 miles of levees and other protection structures lies a city that is an average of five feet below sea level, the second-lowest spot in the nation after Death Valley.

When Jean Baptiste le Moyne, sieur de Bienville, founded New Orleans in 1718, he built the trading settlement on a natural levee of alluvial silt next to the Mississippi, 4.4 feet above sea level. As the city grew, neighborhoods expanded in the only direction they could—north toward Lake Pontchartrain. The six miles of land between the river and the lake was a pestilential cypress swamp used for hunting and portage. Over the decades, the land, some of which is lower than the floor of the lake, was drained and reclaimed by digging a network of drainage canals and installing huge steam-driven paddlewheels to push the periodic floodwaters over a weir and into the lake. Gradually, the bog became habitable. Even then, waterborne tragedies were constant.

Yellow fever epidemics decimated New Orleans throughout the 1800s, the work of a mosquito that bred in the ubiquitous gutters, alleys, and fetid pools that never seemed to dry up. The Yellow Fever Epidemic of 1853 killed 11,000 people, 5 percent of the city's population. In a chilling foreshadowing of the images wrought by Katrina 152 years later, the novelist and journalist George Washington Cable wrote, "The streets became heavy with mud, the air stifling with bad odors, and the whole town a perfect Constantinople for foulness." The city was, one witness told Cable, "a theater of horrors."

But the most constant reminder of the city's precarious existence came from regular springtime river floods and late-summer hurricanes. Katrina wasn't the first catastrophic flood; news accounts dating back to 1735 describe 27 serious floods in New Orleans and its environs. Levee breaches were common in the early days. Observed Mark Twain in 1883, "There is nothing but that frail breastwork of earth between the people and destruction."

After repeated levee raisings, the river dikes today are adequate to protect the New Orleans metropolitan area. The city's flood nightmare has always been its vulnerability to a storm surge approaching from its northern boundary—Lake Pontchartrain. The French named the lake in 1699 for the maritime minister in Paris. But the Choctaw had a more accurate name: "Okwata," the wide water. The brackish, oval-shaped lake is huge, at 630 square miles, and shallow, with an average depth of only 13 feet, making it particularly susceptible to flooding. A major hurricane bearing down on New Orleans would push a mass of water before it, and the hydraulics of southeast Louisiana would provide multiple portals into the lake—which is exactly what happened on August 29.

For days before landfall, the awesome storm had been shouldering the gulf ahead of it and quietly elevating the lake level. When Katrina finally roared ashore, her wind field shoved billions of gallons from Breton, Mississippi, and Chandeleur sounds toward the city from the east. Water gushed into the lake through two narrow inlets, Chef Menteur Pass and the Rigolets strait, at a flow calculated at 450,000 cubic feet of water per second—imagine the Mississippi River pouring directly into Lake Pontchartrain. By the time Katrina passed, the Wide Water was nine feet higher than normal.

Meanwhile, east of the city, a 25-foot storm surge pushed Lake Borgne into St. Bernard Parish and New Orleans East and overtopped the levees of the Mississippi River Gulf Outlet, a misbegotten and little-used navigation canal. Water cascaded into the Lower Ninth Ward through a breach in the eastern edge of the Industrial Canal.

Neptune had risen.

The storm moved north into Mississippi, where it killed more than 225 people and obliterated the coast. Hurricane winds spinning counterclockwise hooked south and rammed the engorged lake hard against the levees. Poorly constructed concrete flood walls atop the earthen dikes along the London Avenue Canal and the 17th Street Canal ruptured. These outfall canals normally drain storm water out of the city, but when they crevassed, they became spigots into the heart of the city.

A team of experts would conclude the flood walls failed, in part, because protective sheet piling along the levees was not driven deep enough to keep water from undermining the soft, unstable delta soil. Investigative forensic engineering teams would later call it the costliest engineering mistake in American history.

As the lake hemorrhaged into the city, the landscape returned to the state in which Bienville found it. Water reclaimed the 78 percent of the city that lies below sea level. Eight out of 10 houses were submerged up to an average depth of 5.2 feet, with some areas under 20 feet of water. This surpassed by far the damage done by the last catastrophic hurricane in memory, Betsy in 1965.

The flood did not damage the city's most fabled structures in the French Quarter, Garden District, Tremé, Faubourg Marigny, and large sections of Uptown. But it enveloped many of the unsung landmarks: the black and yellow home of Antoine "Fats" Domino in the Lower Ninth; the St. Roche fish market on St. Claude; the residence of the late jazz guitarist Danny Barker in Gentilly; Liuzza's Restaurant and Bar in Midtown; and the Dew Drop Inn on LaSalle Street, once "the South's Swankiest Night Spot."

Neptune had won.

In a quiet neighborhood in Baton Rouge near the university where he used to work, 61-year-old Joseph Suhayda watched the mighty storm's approach on television with a sickening feeling. The veteran coastal oceanographer had studied hurricane behavior for 30 years, developed computer simulations of the Big One, and helped New Orleans develop its emergency hurricane plan. He thought, "It's following the script."

Suhayda was proud of the accuracy of his computer models that predicted the effect of a huge storm surge approaching from the lake. "But I still can't translate the emotionless modeling of water coming into the city to the reality of people trapped on their rooftops," he said. "The human toll is 10 times what I anticipated."

On Wednesday, the water and the crisis deepen. It's morning, and we're sitting in the truck downtown, staring at water that now covers Loyola and is inching up Howard Avenue.

Storm refugees, nearly all of them black, are on the move throughout the city. And they are *refugees*, as in, people fleeing misfortune and seeking refuge. NPR and other news organizations caved to pressure from critics who did not like the word. We substituted "evacuees." Some listeners thought "refugee" carried a pejorative foreign connotation, something that happens in Sudan or Somalia but never the United States. That's precisely why I preferred the term. I hoped it would shock people into realizing that an American city had sunk to Third-World conditions.

Hawke and I hop out of the truck to interview a ragged string of refugees walking up Howard on the way to the Superdome, trailed by an obese woman in stretch shorts. "I got a bad heart. I ain't got no business travelin' like this," she says.

A woman with matted hair in a Tweety Bird T-shirt says, "We slept all night on the bridge. They say go across the river and the buses will pick us up. Now they're turnin' us all around. We need somebody who knows what's goin' *on*!"

I ask more questions, but they want answers. Where to get a meal? Where to find a bus?

"Tell the truth," a young man in a Bob Marley T-shirt asks in exasperation. "Y'all care about us?"

"Of *course* we do," Hawke replies.

"Well, *help* us," he says sharply. "They got people layin' up there on the bridge dyin'. . . . I know y'all want our story, but we need help!"

We don't know where they should go, either. And we're worried that if we hand out the little food and water we have in the truck, we'll cause a scene. Still, he makes a powerful point: We need a story; he needs a rescue.

A couple of weeks later, a listener will e-mail NPR and ask, "What about the demands of suffering humanity? Do you ever feel that jour-

nalism is an inadequate response to the tragedies you report on?"
Other listeners suggest we should have turned our sat phone over to
the cops after they lost communication.

The role of journalist as detached chronicler or part-time rescuer
will be discussed intensely after Katrina. Purists argue that journalists
should never participate in a story—period. We bear witness to history;
we don't step into it. But it's not that simple. We don't leave our humanity at home when we cover a disaster. Anytime I, as a journalist, record
a person in misery and then walk away, I feel like the photographer who
queasily described his role, saying, "We came to take our trophies and
left." There's something unbecoming about that behavior, particularly if
we can offer a small kindness without neglecting our job.

Later in the week, Hawke and I hand out water and snacks to
individual refugees we encounter, and the NPR crew gives four desperate Canadian tourists a ride to Baton Rouge. I heard of other journalists using their news boats to rescue people. I believe you do what you
can, but you never let go of the story. And on this story, in particular,
journalists will perform a service by being on the ground and in the
water to show the world and our own government the terrible conditions in New Orleans.

The unrelenting sun turns the morning into a sauna. I crank up
the Ford's A/C and think sadly about the people stuck in the sweltering
Superdome or sitting on their rooftops. This is the same heat wave that
warmed the gulf and created the monster hurricane. Our world is heat-
ing up. There could well be more Katrinas in future summers. But at
the moment, they've got to fix this one.

In the Rose Garden, President Bush ticks off all the federal aid
bound for New Orleans: 400 trucks transporting 5.4 million meals,
13.4 million liters of water, 10,400 tarps, 3.4 million pounds of ice, 144
generators, 135,000 blankets. It probably sounds reassuring to people

everywhere but here, where they know the truth. The relief effort—if there is one—has fallen into chaos. No one is in charge. Storm survivors are adrift in the gulf of New Orleans. The city needs everything—food, water, buses, boats, doctors, soldiers, ice, and body bags. And what does Governor Blanco do? She calls for a statewide Day of Prayer.

I zigzag through fallen limbs along St. Charles Avenue, famed for its Mardi Gras parades and formerly shady oaks. When I spot more refugees wading up the street, I pull onto the streetcar tracks and kill the engine. We climb out and introduce ourselves to Latoya Solomon, a 24-year-old hotel employee who's walking with 12 members of her family, from a tot happily splashing along the pavement to a grim old woman in an orange life vest. As soon as my first question is out, Solomon starts to rant. "The water's off, the light's off, everything's flooded, everything's soakin' wet, we can't eat, we can't cook, stores ain't open. We thirsty. What? *What?* I don't see nobody tryin' to help us. Everybody just walkin' around lookin' lonesome. This ain't gonna *work*," she says. I wish I could put her on live with the president.

It's early afternoon when we start to put our story together. I park the truck next to the Hilton and plug my laptop into the cigarette lighter. The cab is hot, so I move to an alcove in the outside wall and try to write fast, as the midday subtropical sun creeps up my legs and onto my chest.

Hawke goes into the hotel to get us lunch. Of all the hotels that stayed open through the storm, the Hilton may be the best spot, and we're lucky to be here. The kitchen had stockpiled barbecue, red beans and rice, egg rolls, gumbo, and other dishes for a huge political party that was canceled just before the storm. Twice a day, the hotel staff serves it up to the ravenous guests. The employees—unwashed, fatigued, many whose own homes had flooded—are unfailingly polite.

I watch workers running up the stairwell with food plates for elderly guests.

How I dread the stairwell. People have left plates of old food in the corners and allowed their dogs to defecate on the steps. Death by heart attack seems imminent. Every time I start the long climb, it seems, there's an overweight woman stopped between floors, breathing heavily and muttering, "Lord have mercy. *Walk* with me, Jesus." We check and recheck our gear every morning before we leave the rooms to be sure we won't have to dash back up the hellish stairwell for spare batteries.

Hawke returns with two plates of fried chicken and mashed potatoes, the first hot meal we've had in three days. In a town renowned for its cuisine, I've never enjoyed anything as much as that Hilton chicken.

After lunch, now in a full sunbath, we start blocking out the story. My editor has given me a length of 4½ minutes. Hawke listens to the interviews we collected in the morning and feeds me quotes, which I incorporate into my script. She's a seasoned pro, and the work goes quickly. We constantly monitor battery life because our equipment— laptops, cell phones, BlackBerrys, and satellite phones—must be charged on the car battery.

When the story is finished, we try to call an editor in Washington for an edit. The cell network is down. On her BlackBerry, Hawke text-messages the deputy senior national desk editor, David Sweeney, who notifies record central (RC) to expect a call on the sat phone. We race up to the roof of the garage, fire up the sat phone, and edit with senior national desk editor Ellen Weiss—trying not to think about how it's costing the network $8.25 a minute.

I never take this marvelous machine for granted. Sixteen years earlier, during Hurricane Hugo, I sent my tape to Washington by holding my headphones to the mouthpiece of a pay phone in the lobby of the

Holiday Inn in Charleston, South Carolina. Satellite phones still seem like sorcery to me. You locate the Atlantic Ocean Region Inmarsat satellite and punch in RC's number. A red light blinks on, and the next thing you know, you can send and receive high-fidelity, broadcast-quality sound anywhere on the globe.

Reading off my laptop, I voice the script into a microphone hooked up to an analog-to-digital converter. Hawke plays actualities (audio quotes) of the refugees on Howard Avenue and ambient sound of their feet splashing in the water. A producer in Washington will assemble the story elements per my instructions, and we pray it comes in at the promised length.

On a big breaking story like Katrina, there's never Miller Time. As soon as the RC engineer tells us the piece is filed, we break down the sat phone, pack it up, climb back in the pickup, and head back onto the streets for more reporting.

With no help on the way and no one in charge, New Orleans is descending into panic. A young announcer on WWL, whom we've heard on the air for three days straight, is growing despondent. "We're fighting an unprecedented war," he says in an exhausted monotone, "and we wonder if our city can be saved."

City leaders, in a state of shock and fatigue, succumb to wild rumors and primal fears. Police superintendent Eddie Compass Jr. tells Oprah Winfrey about "little babies getting raped" in the Superdome. Nagin decries the "hooligans killing people, raping people." City council president Oliver M. Thomas Jr. wonders on the radio, "Maybe God's going to cleanse us."

I like the answer a woman gave to a *New York Times* reporter when told about preachers attributing the flood to God's wrath: "If he wanted to punish the Gulf Coast, then how come Bourbon Street wasn't touched?"

Young men zip down deserted boulevards in vehicles filled with stolen liquor, TVs, computers, guns, and other booty. On Magazine Street, the Radio Shack, Harry's Ace Hardware, and A&P are broken into. Specialty shops such as LaBardin Chandeliers, the Magic Toy Box, and the Dog-O-Mat do-it-yourself dog wash are untouched. At the Everything Shoppe on Canal Street, looters haul off Hard Lemonade, Bacardi Limón, and Blackened Voodoo Beer, but they leave the feathered Mardi Gras masks, "Will Cook for Sex" aprons, and grotesquely smiling Satchmo figurines.

Bob Rue, the gray-ponytailed owner of Sarouk Oriental Rugs on St. Charles, paints on his establishment in large letters, "DON'T TRY. I AM SLEEPING INSIDE WITH A BIG DOG, AN UGLY WOMAN, TWO SHOTGUNS, AND A CLAW HAMMER." Rue later told me he had none of the above—in fact, he was sleeping with a .38 at his girlfriend's house—but the sign worked and his shop was safe.

On Constance Street in front of Audubon Zoo, whose animals all survived, we stop to chat with a friendly lieutenant in a state police cruiser. It's unclear whether he's on duty or what exactly he's doing. He's wearing a T-shirt with a 9 mm pistol stuffed in the waist of his athletic shorts, and he says he's going to check on his sister's house.

He glances at my pickup and tells us to be careful about carjackings. "Are y'all armed?" he asks. "Because y'all need to be."

As we pull away from the park, I say to Hawke, "I wish we had a security guard with a big gun to ride in the back of the truck. Did you see that big rent-a-cop ABC has? ABC also has its own boat. Damn, I wish we had a boat."

The NOPD has imploded. The flood has claimed 575 cars, 7 district stations, the armory, evidence room, crime lab, jail, and the homes of 8 out of 10 officers on the 1,500-member force. Radios are dead, and officers communicate in line-of-sight fashion—like Wild West posses.

Within the week, more than 200 officers desert. Two more shoot themselves in suicides. Some join hoodlums in taking loot and stealing cars. Two *Times-Picayune* reporters witness cops at a Wal-Mart hauling off a 27-inch flat-screen TV in a shopping cart. Most of the New Orleans police, however, distinguish themselves by staying on the job around the clock in the turbulent days after the storm.

Police presence seems improvised. A cop with an assault rifle slung around his neck directs traffic on a meter maid's scooter. Two officers stand guard in a boat bobbing in front of City Hall. A commander directs rescue operations from a folding table set up in the driveway of Harrah's casino.

The bizarre becomes normal. WWL TV reporter Jonathan Betz watches a woman wading near Poydras and Loyola streets, pulling the body of her dead husband on a floating door behind her.

There are countless heroes. Officers with the NOPD, US Coast Guard, and Louisiana Department of Wildlife and Fisheries save thousands of lives in house-to-house rescues by boat and helicopter. Employees of the New Orleans Sewerage and Water Board stay on the job day and night to get the pumps started to dry the city. The New Mexico Disaster Medical Assistance Team, working in deplorable conditions, saves lives inside the Superdome. And the Cajun armada arrives. Men who could paddle a pirogue before they could ride a bicycle stream into town, pulling bass boats and flat-bottom bateaus.

On the corner of Poydras and Baronne, we meet Marty Bordelon, a bull-necked 55-year-old offshore oil industry instructor wearing rubber boots and a camo jumpsuit. He says he towed his boat from Moreauville, 150 miles away. "You always see a disaster and think, 'Well, if I could just help somebody.' My wife told me yesterday, she says, 'Marty, if you go and help one person,' she says, 'it's worth it.' I say, 'Well then, we goin'.'"

But rescue is only half the work. Once the survivors are deposited on high ground, they have no place to go. With the Superdome and the adjacent New Orleans Arena full to capacity, unplanned refugee camps spring up all over. Thousands of people assemble on the searing asphalt intersection of Causeway Boulevard and I-10 in Metairie. In neighboring St. Bernard Parish, some 1,500 residents await rescue at the Chalmette ferry landing. And a multitude is gathering at the downtown Convention Center in the mistaken belief that buses will pick them up. Hour by hour, these accumulations of people grow in size and wretchedness.

Despite these disturbing images, it's important to note that it could have been worse. Officials consider the prestorm evacuation a success. Ninety percent of the region's residents left. Hurricane planners had feared as many as 60,000 lives could be lost when the Big One hit New Orleans. That didn't happen.

Why didn't more residents leave? Much has been made of the fact that in this city of nearly 500,000, where one in four is poor, 100,000 residents reportedly didn't have vehicles. Less attention has been paid to the thousands of swamped vehicles that were visible throughout the city, including those lining the streets surrounding the Superdome. Of the dozens of evacuees I interviewed inside and outside New Orleans, not one told me, "I wanted to leave, but I couldn't."

Many ignored the mayor's call for a mandatory evacuation the day before the storm. They stayed to guard their property, care for an elderly person, or "ride it out" like their daddy always did—or because it was just too damned much trouble to evacuate. During a previous evacuation, perhaps they'd been stuck on the highway for eight hours, only to watch the hurricane miss the Crescent City, and they said, never again. For many, their choice to ride out Katrina was the worst decision of their lives.

❖

We park the F-150, which I've come to think of as a sort of mother ship that will protect us from all harm, in the circular driveway in front of the Hilton. There's commotion on the sidewalk—people pulling luggage; cops giving orders. Concerned about the city's degenerating sanitation and growing anarchy, the hotel announces it is closing, and all guests will be bused out of town.

"We're not staying in this city tonight," I tell Hawke.

She runs into the Hilton, finds a working pay phone, calls Sweeney, and asks him to find a place for all four of us. He's been monitoring reports of the city's slide into lawlessness and is clearly relieved that we're leaving. "Get the fuck out," he tells her. "I'll call our station in Baton Rouge and see if they can put you up."

Two blocks away, an invisible drama is unfolding behind the tall concrete walls of the Aquarium of the Americas—the number-one tourist attraction in Louisiana. A storm-rider crew has been up for four days, trying to save 10,000 sea creatures that live inside. The emergency generator is running out of diesel and having mechanical problems; and the oxygenation and filtration systems for a million gallons of water, both salt and fresh, are slowly failing. Nine staffers desperately try to keep the water livable by dropping oxygen diffusers into the tanks. They stop feeding the big animals so they won't produce so much ammonia in the deteriorating water. But it's not enough. On Wednesday, a police SWAT commander tells them water in the streets is rising and the city is out of control. Fearing for its safety, the crew packs up and convoys toward Baton Rouge the same afternoon as we do.

"The game plan was, we thought we'd be back up and running in three days or so," James Arnold tells me afterward. He's a marine biologist who slept on an air mattress next to the sea-otter exhibit. "But how do you design an emergency system to run for two weeks? The generator's not supposed to run for more than 72 hours. It was hard. Really depressing."

After the storm riders leave, ammonia levels soar. As more fish die, the water grows exponentially more toxic. The goliath grouper and the nurse, brown, and sand tiger sharks in the popular Gulf of Mexico exhibit perish, along with most of the other fish in the famed aquarium. When the staff returns four days later, they will rejoice that the sea otters, penguins, sea dragons, clownfish, and King Midas the green sea turtle somehow survived.

I find the entrance to the Crescent City Connection bridge and floor it. There's a stripped and abandoned White Fleet cab parked next to the ramp. On the shoulder, a man with a backpack hitchhikes frantically. I watch him flail his arms and curse me in the rearview mirror. Speeding out of the shattered city, I imagine a scene from a bad disaster movie: *Escape from New Orleans*. Who thought it would come to this?

All four of us—me, Allen, Muturi, and Hawke—convoy to Baton Rouge and hit a health club for showers, a Cajun restaurant for dinner, and a Wal-Mart for pillows and blankets. That night, we feel incredibly lucky to be sleeping on the carpet of the member station, WRKF.

In Crawford earlier on Wednesday, President Bush cuts short his summer vacation and announces he'll return to Washington to coordinate relief efforts. *Air Force One* makes a low-altitude pass over New Orleans and the Mississippi Gulf Coast; the president peers out the window and tells an aide, "It's devastating."

In Washington, they're patting themselves on the back. Michael Chertoff, secretary of the Department of Homeland Security, declares Katrina an "incident of national significance" and comments, "We are extremely pleased with the response that every element of the federal government, all of our federal partners, have made to this terrible tragedy."

In Baton Rouge, FEMA chief Michael Brown's press secretary, Sharon Worthy, e-mails colleagues: "It is very important that time is allowed for Mr. Brown to eat dinner. . . . Restaurants are getting busy. He needs much more than 20 or 30 minutes. We now have traffic to encounter to get to and from a location of his choice."

In New Orleans, FEMA's Bahamonde e-mails a response: "OH MY GOD!!!!!!!! . . . Just tell her that I just ate an MRE and crapped in the hallway of the Superdome along with 30,000 other close friends so I understand her concern about busy restaurants."

On Thursday morning, under a gray, rainy sky, we fill the tank in Baton Rouge, grab breakfast at an IHOP, check our equipment and food supplies, and jump back on the interstate. A state trooper with a buzz cut and an underbite stops Hawke and me at a roadblock on the outskirts of New Orleans. He scans our press credentials and waves us through, drawling, "Go on, git outta here."

As soon as we cross the Crescent City Connection, we see hordes of people waiting for rescue on the elevated expressway. I take the Camp Street exit, drive into downtown, and see more people wandering the streets. They stare at us as we pass. There's recognition in their faces that we're white and have transportation and they're black and on foot. There's also a look of uncomprehension. Why, three days after the storm, has no one come to help them?

It is now apparent that the city—if it still is a city—has disintegrated. Civil order has melted away. The licentious, devil-may-care Big Easy, where it was fun to break the rules, now has no rules whatsoever. We have entered the twilight zone. We are witnesses to an epic calamity.

Homeland Security refuses to let the Red Cross into New Orleans because it's too dangerous. FEMA water rescues are suspended because of reports of gunfire.

In the absence of information, rumors spin out of control: They've blown the levees to save the French Quarter. A toxic cloud from a flaming oil tank is drifting over the West Bank. Hundreds of inmates from the Orleans Parish Prison have been released. Marauding gangs are breaking into Garden District mansions to slash family portraits. None of them is true, but anything seems possible.

We stop by the Loyola Street entrance to the Superdome and see that buses have finally begun arriving to carry storm victims out of town. Exhausted, limping evacuees from inside that hellhole are boarding spiffy tourist buses bound for the Astrodome in Houston, 350 miles away. Finally, some good news. I spot an aide to the police superintendent—he shoulders an assault rifle and looks like he could bench-press 300 pounds—who agrees to talk to me not for attribution.

"Where the fuck are the feds?" he asks. "There's not enough National Guard. They're all in Iraq. We can't stop the looting. The situation is changing hourly. I want to know where the goddamn government is."

The police are so confused they're telling people the Ernest N. Morial Convention Center is "an impromptu collection point" for buses. As a result, refugees have been congregating there for days. We get reports they're growing restive and desperate. Hawke and I decide to check it out.

Fearing a carjacking, we park the truck near the now-deserted Hilton and walk two blocks to the sprawling structure. The convention center is a mile-long, orange-and-tan building with a giant fleur-de-lis logo and more than three million square feet of floor space. The last customer, the game show *Wheel of Fortune*, hastily wrapped up its shoot and got out of town on Saturday before the storm. The first refugees began showing up there the day after Katrina. As we approach under a light rain, a sea of people spreads out on the sidewalk and across the street.

The crowd, which authorities later estimate at 15,000 to 20,000, sits in orange-cushioned folding chairs, surrounded by hastily rescued belongings. They're gloomy and furious at their abandonment. Hawke's slim shotgun microphone is like a magic wand that stimulates an outpouring of lamentations.

An unidentified man reeking of stale sweat yells, "They got people dyin' in here. They got elderly people with heart trouble, high blood pressure, sugar diabetes. Ain't nobody sent nothin'!"

"Where's the Red Cross at?" says Kevin Goodman, a Mardi Gras Indian chief from the Seventh Ward. "We haven't eaten in three, four days! My family's about to fall out."

"It's chaotic. Everyone is panicking. It's just awful. We're overcrowded. It's filthy, very filthy inside, and we're just trying to survive," says Joyce Matthews from New Orleans East.

People are speaking on top of one another. A woman who gives her name as Victory Wells tugs on my sleeve. "The children don't have food or nothin'. We're just like scavengers. Can you all please help us, in the name of Jesus?"

"That's what we're here for, to get the message out," I say.

"You're gonna get out," Hawke adds.

The refugees look at us dubiously. They describe conditions inside the cavernous center as "pure hell"—worse, indeed, than the flooded neighborhoods they escaped. I walk inside. The carpet outside the stopped-up bathroom is slick with sewage. Garbage is strewn everywhere. Babies cry. Old people are pale and motionless; some appear to be dying. It's later learned that two out of every three storm fatalities were elderly.

An aged couple sits together in the middle of an exhibit hall. The wife is spooning something from a Meals Ready to Eat (MRE) packet into her husband's mouth. He's slumped over in a wheelchair. When I ask them how they're doing, she looks up with unfocused eyes. "We can't talk to you; we're waiting for FEMA. We have to talk to FEMA," she says over and over.

As I learn in later interviews, young men from housing projects, armed and drunk on looted liquor, have established territory in the exhibit halls and are making mayhem. Some hoard food and water to sell for money or trade for sex. Refugees tell us the gangsters molest girls and shoot their pistols at night. Women say they're terrified and only travel through the darkened halls in groups.

At one point, young thugs hot-wire a golf cart and careen around the building, repeatedly ramming a group of men from Mary Queen of Vietnam Catholic Church, who've encircled their women and children for protection. "But we didn't want to fight with them, we didn't want to mess with them, too many of them," Ronnie Nguyen, a computer technician, tells me later.

Rev. Toby Nelson, a Presbyterian minister from Hayward, California, who was chaplain with an emergency medical team inside the Superdome, told me later, "We saw that when people don't have food or water or sanitation, it takes only about 48 hours for civil order to break down. I can only compare it to *Lord of the Flies*, where gangs were the only sense of order. It seems like the beast that is resident in each of us was released."

Outnumbered and overpowered, police officers patrol outside the convention center during the day but make infrequent trips inside.

Even the military hides from the unruly crowd. Two engineering batallions with the Louisiana Army National Guard, who've been tasked with clearing roads, have barricaded themselves in an exhibit hall at the back of the facility. Fearing a riot, the guardsmen pulled out a few hours before we arrive on Thursday.

With their city gone, a society of sorts emerges among the forgotten convention center refugees. And the decent far outnumber the depraved.

Some old people who cannot open plastic MRE packets or wipe the human waste off themselves are assisted by strangers. Others make crosses and raise them over the crowd as if to say, according to one witness, "This is our area. We're about church. We ain't about no trouble." When the assemblage grows hopeless, a woman named Anita Roach, choir director at the New Jerusalem Missionary Baptist Church, leads the crowd in spirituals, as chronicled movingly by *Times-Picayune* reporter Brian Thevenot.

> *When the storm of life is raging*
> *Stand by me,*
> *When the world is tossing me*
> *Like a ship upon the sea*
> *Thou who rulest the wind and water*
> *Stand by me.*

People protect one another. "I worked in the jailhouse for 15 years, and I never seen that much violence for them three nights," Derek McKay, a corrections officer at the Orleans Parish jail, tells me later. "We had a plan if they came over there; we wouldn't let them hurt none of them children and old people. We'd do whatever was necessary."

People feed one another. Families share what bottled water and juice and snacks they can scrounge. A group of men breaks into the kitchen of the Marriott across the street to cook eggs, grits, and sausage and hand out plates to old people, women, and children. Others fix smoked sausage on a charcoal grill on the sidewalk, all of it filched from Wal-Mart, to feed their neighbors.

Many take advantage of the lawlessness and help themselves to other goodies. A man walks through the convention center announcing, "Stores are open; it's time to go shopping," and people hustle over to the Riverwalk Marketplace. In short order, they return wearing new outfits and new shoes. A man in the corner auctions off LSU football jerseys. Another pads past in Homer Simpson slippers. New Chanel and Christian Dior outfits appear incongruously on women who waded through dirty floodwaters.

We hear stories of rampant rapes and killings, about "beaucoup bodies" stacked in a walk-in freezer in the center. Show them to me, I ask. We're directed to the sidewalk on the northern end of the building where the bodies of two old people have been deposited. The form of a small woman wrapped in a plaid blanket slumps in a wheelchair; a white-shrouded man lies curled on the sidewalk. Scores of evacuees tell me about a young or teenaged girl who was raped and had her throat cut. Three people say they saw the body themselves. Weeks later, the official death toll from the convention center is set at four, only one of which is a homicide. The body of a girl with her throat slit never turns up. The authorities dismiss widespread accounts of murders as "emotional hallucinations."

With bestial conditions and no help, refugees are at a loss to understand why they were sent to the convention center in the first place. "What they brought us over here for to kill us? That's what it seems," says 63-year-old Adrina Washington, holding an umbrella in the drizzling rain and staring at the two dead old people.

Perhaps the evacuation debacle unleashes old suspicions among the mostly black refugees, a collective memory of misery and mistreatment. The New Orleans slave pens. Black codes. Klan justice. Whites only. Their fears are not fiction. Upriver, in the aftermath of the Great Mississippi Flood of 1927, thousands of black delta residents were herded onto the levees and held there in squalid conditions so the planters wouldn't lose their labor source.

Hawke and I walk back to the truck, stunned at all we have seen and heard. "It's unbelievable," she says. "John, you and I could have gone to Wal-Mart and gotten food for those people."

"I guess you could say the City That Care Forgot has become the City the Nation Forgot," I say.

Miraculously, I get a cell-phone call through to *All Things Considered*. I feed some notes to a producer, who relays them to cohost Robert Siegel, who happens to be interviewing Chertoff at that moment. Chertoff is doing what federal officials do every day in Washington: trying to convince the nation that Responsible Men Are in Charge So You Mustn't Worry. But it isn't washing.

Siegel: "We are hearing from our reporter—and he's on another line right now—thousands of people at the convention center in New Orleans with no food, zero."

Chertoff: "As I say, I'm telling you that we are getting food and water to areas where people are staging. And you know, the one thing about an episode like this is if you talk to someone and you get a rumor or you get someone's anecdotal version of something, I think it's dangerous to extrapolate it all over the place. . . ."

Siegel: "But sorry, Mr. Secretary, when you say we shouldn't listen to rumors, these are things coming from reporters who have not only covered many, many hurricanes, they've covered wars and refugee camps. These aren't rumors. They're seeing thousands of people there."

Chertoff: "Well . . . actually, I have not heard a report of thousands of people in the convention center who don't have food or water. . . ."

After the interview, I go on the air with Siegal to narrate in stark detail what we've just witnessed.

After his interview with NPR, Chertoff turns to an aide and, according to *Newsweek*, says, "What the hell is going on with the convention center?" After some ground truthing, he learns the crowd has swelled from 1,500—his initial report—to some 15,000. This, he says, was his lowest moment during a dismal week.

Two hours after the Siegel-Chertoff exchange, Hawke and I are sitting in a boat as it putters over parking meters on Gravier Street. It's being used to rescue premature babies and dialysis patients from flooded Charity and University Hospitals. I'll never forget the image of a boatload of nurses in soiled green uniforms cradling tiny, swaddled infants, all floating quietly along the street. The irrepressible Cajun boatman jokes about salvaging some of the floating furniture he's poking through: "I *know* I can use that in my fish camp."

Hawke's cell phone rings. It's Sweeney. "Chertoff's office called ATC after the two-way and told them Homeland Security has confirmed conditions at the convention center. They said they're sending choppers to airdrop food and water this afternoon."

At that moment, I love being a journalist. Sometimes we do make a difference. Suddenly, I don't feel so useless.

Late that afternoon, we pull onto the Tchoupitoulas Street ramp to the bridge and again flee the ruined city. Looters have torched a mall beside the West Bank Expressway, and black smoke billows into the pale coastal sky. Stripped vehicles are abandoned on the shoulder. Shopping carts and suitcases litter the roadway. Walkers beg for rides. In a matter of four days, this scene has become routine.

❖

The cumulative impact of the story has been building in all of us. We're emotionally frayed. That night in Baton Rouge, I retrieve a message on my cell phone from my 11-year-old daughter, Helen. She has a cold, and she stayed home from school and watched the news on CNN. "Dawi, you're so brave. Don't you wish you'd brought the canoe? I'm worried about you and I love you. I want you to come home soon." Her voice is small, innocent, and beautiful. That's when I lose it. I say a prayer of thanks that my family is high and dry and safe in Austin.

The next day, Friday, the fifth day after the storm, help finally arrives. Army Lieutenant General Russel Honore, newly appointed commander of the relief effort, rides to the convention center at the head of a convoy of camouflage-green supply trucks carrying food, water, and troops. Buses soon follow.

"I've never seen anything more glorious in my life," councilwoman Clarkson tells me later. "Oh, it was like God had appeared."

On WWL, Nagin lets the feds have it. "Now get off your asses and do something, and let's fix the biggest goddamn crisis in the history of this country."

Bush tours the hurricane-hit areas and acknowledges for the first time that "the results are not acceptable." Nevertheless, he tells his FEMA chief the same day, "Brownie, you're doin' a heckuva job."

Five months later, a bipartisan House Select Committee investigating the federal response to Katrina concludes, "The failure of initiative cost lives, prolonged suffering, and left all Americans justifiably concerned our government is no better prepared to protect its people than it was before 9/11. . . ." The report singles out the White House, which was "overcome by the fog of war."

The crisis is ending, but the weirdness is just beginning.

Chapter 2

UNDER THE DRAGON'S WING
IN IRAQ

THE GREAT WAR MACHINE stirred to life. President George W. Bush had already given his Texas-style ultimatum to Saddam Hussein and his two sons, Uday and Qusay: You've got 48 hours to get out of town or we're comin' in after you. In expectation of the Iraqi leader's defiant response, the First Marine Division was making its way to a staging area in the northern Kuwaiti desert only a couple miles shy of the Iraq border. Six marines rode in the back of a Humvee with me, brooding.

"I wonder what they'll call this thing?" asked one.

"I don't know, but I bet it's got 'noble' or 'fury' in it," said another.

The motorcade rumbled northward through the wasteland toward an illusory enemy. The night of March 20, 2003, was cold, impenetrably dark, and foreign—at least to me. The headlights fell on a camel-crossing sign beside the highway. The ride seemed interminable. Wasn't Kuwait smaller than West Virginia? Something was wrong. Suddenly, in front of us, headlights illuminated the 10-foot sand berm that delineates the border between Kuwait and Iraq. Bravo Convoy was about to invade Iraq 24 hours before the start of the war.

"Where in the hell are we?" a voice in a vehicle ahead called out.

With the electric fence separating the hostile neighbors now in plain sight, Master Gunnery Sergeant Steve Schweitzer, riding beside me in the Humvee, took charge. Schweitzer, an excitable Oregonian, was the bandmaster of the First Marine Division Band, in which I was embedded.

"We are the fucking *band!*" he yelled, sounding like the road manager from *This Is Spinal Tap*.

In an instant, saxophonists, trumpeters, trombonists, clarinetists, drummers, and tuba players sprinted into the moonless desert and threw themselves onto the sand, M-16s at the ready. This was a true band of brothers. Gears groaned as the war wagons performed a hasty U-turn. A corporal in the lead vehicle, we later learned, had missed the drivers' briefing.

"How close did we just come to starting the war?" I asked Schweitzer, as a chill wind whipped our faces.

"Close enough to smell the Iraqis' aftershave," he said, grinning.

When I left Austin in early March to link up with the marines in Kuwait, my 11-year-old son, Grant, had on the floor of his room a toy journalist. It was a special edition G.I. Joe in the likeness of Ernie Pyle, the famed Scripps Howard war correspondent. The movable figure came with its own folding table, a little plastic typewriter, and a khaki jacket with a "Combat Correspondent" patch. Only the flask was missing. When Grant arranged his elaborate battle scenes with other G.I. Joes, he was always careful to place Ernie safely out of the line of fire, with his Smith-Corona in his lap. It was Grant's way, I thought, to convince himself that his own father would be safe covering the impending war with Iraq.

Correspondents who covered World War II operated under a set of rules and expectations out of a different century. They dressed in khaki officers' uniforms and had their dispatches vetted by the Office of Censorship. Patriotism was implicit in their work. The United States and its allies confronted an evil that everyone could agree on. How could an American journalist not want to contribute to the fight against fascism?

Sixty years later, the Pentagon's unprecedented decision to embed some 600 reporters with the US military as it prepared a preemptive overthrow of the Iraqi government was an attempt to reprise that noble theme. From our perspective, we would all get to be Ernie Pyle on the road to Baghdad. More important, the arrangement was a vast improvement over the stifling restrictions imposed on reporters' movements during the Persian Gulf War. The embedding experiment also brilliantly achieved the public relations objectives of the Pentagon. War planners hoped the real-time images that CNN and Fox News beamed from the battlefield would counter Iraq's version of the war transmitted by Al-Jazeera to the Arab world.

The Pentagon implicitly understood what happens when journalists are inserted into war-fighting units. People who share adversity grow closer. We would sleep in the sand together, eat bad food together, and ride out sandstorms together. David Wood, the veteran national security correspondent for Newhouse News, cautions new combat reporters that the hardest thing about covering war is not the danger of incoming mortar rounds: "It's remembering at all times that you're not one of them."

For years I had watched military operations from the sidelines, embedded in the communities that were victimized by war—in Guatemala, Colombia, Afghanistan, Kosovo. Finally, I had an opportunity to witness military science from the inside—way inside. By the end of my six-week stint with the marines, I wound up questioning whether embedding had become shorthand for "in bed with."

The official press center for journalists covering Operation Iraqi

Freedom (it didn't have "noble" or "fury" in it after all) was located inside the Kuwait Hilton Resort overlooking the warm waters of the Persian Gulf. They couldn't have picked a setting that contrasted more with the upcoming battlefield. Every night, journalists and military flaks browsed through an obscenely plentiful buffet of steamed prawns, Gorgonzola cheese, pâté, and chocolate mousse. After dinner, we retired poolside and smoked apple-flavored tobacco from hubble-bubbles. At the hotel Starbucks, elegant Kuwaiti women in head-to-foot black *abayas* lifted their veils to sip lattes. We bought sand goggles from a chic sunglasses boutique in the hotel and attended mandatory preinvasion briefings.

We signed a document to "release, indemnify and hold harmless" the US government. (Fifteen journalists died during the Iraq campaign, but no families sued.) We reluctantly agreed to 50 "ground rules" that included not giving away troop location, not revealing troop strength, and not photographing the faces of dead American troops. We got smallpox vaccinations with the warning that if we scratched the vaccination site and then touched our genitals, we would regret it very, very much. We dumped all brightly colored clothing after hearing the admonition that the enemy operates on the principle "If it looks different, kill it." I tried not to think about the fact that I'm tall.

We learned to call marines grunts, jarheads, or devil dogs—never soldiers—and were made to understand that it was an honor to have drawn this assignment. The First Marine Division is the oldest and most decorated division-size unit in the US Marine Corps (USMC), earning presidential unit citations for its service at Guadalcanal, Peleliu, and Okinawa in World War II and two more in Korea. The marines are an amphibious assault force trained to take beachheads and travel perhaps 50 miles inland. In Iraq, the 23,000 men and women of

1MarDiv would move 400 miles across a desert, farther inland than any marine unit in history.

The invasion plan called for the US Army Fifth Corps to race through the desert west of the Euphrates and the Tigris and attack Baghdad from the south and west. The First Marine Expeditionary Force, of which 1MarDiv was a part, would proceed up a parallel course through ancient Mesopotamia—the land between the rivers—and strike the capital from the east and north. The army and marines were to crush Saddam in a vise. Meanwhile, the British would secure the strategic southern city of Basra.

Other reporters were assigned to scout snipers, artillery, tanks, infantry, and combat engineers. I had drawn the First Marine Division Band. If I had visions of the band playing a stirring march while the infantry attacked, like Santa Anna's troops at the Alamo, Schweitzer dashed my expectations: "In this war we are tactical, not musical," he said. During wartime, the band provides perimeter security for the headquarters batallion. I would be close to the division nerve center. This suited me just fine. First, I didn't want to be at the tip of the spear; I wanted to be somewhere on the shaft. Second, I never cared for glorifying the kill-'em-all-and-let-God-sort-'em-out types. I was with musicians. Having played in bands for years—my instrument, in fact, is the Hohner Marine Band harmonica—I felt right at home.

"Does the fact that you play tuba make you any less lethal?" I asked Sergeant Michael Yager, a 25-year-old tubaist from Portsmouth, New Hampshire.

"Not at all. I'd say it makes me more lethal," he retorted. "Musicians are calculating. We have to make snap decisions, how I'm going to cover up for things and adapt. Same thing in battle."

❖

After Bravo Convoy's false start, US forces launched their "decap-itation" attack against the Iraqis as scheduled. The land invasion was anticlimactic because the initial artillery and air attack had annihi-lated Iraq's meager border defenses. The better-trained Republican Guard divisions lay days ahead on the road to Baghdad. The five reporters embedded in our batallion rode and dozed, the main pastime of mechanized armies on the move.

We traveled mostly in the rear of a seven-ton Oshkosh truck, lying on sandbags and watching the unerring flatness pass by through a raised rear canvas flap. When the convoy stopped long enough for us to scramble out to pee, the surroundings looked like the surface of a strange planet, colorless but for the presence of iridescent green flies, featureless but for the improbable roadside picnic areas. Had they been erected in a burst of goodwill by a civic-spirited official from the Ministry of Trans-portation? I imagined a Shia family sitting on the gay yellow molded benches, grimly chewing kebabs as Saddam's henchmen drained their marshes. Most of the picnic areas were now history, pancaked by 68-ton M1A1 Abrams tanks. The war machine rolled on.

The headquarters batallion created its own atmosphere, its own sovereignty, like a US-flagged vessel in international waters. It was a tent city on wheels that carried with it everything necessary to conduct a modern war, from spare printer cables to communion wafers to a combat psychiatrist. Once we entered Iraq, rules of engagement replaced the rule of law. The conduct of every citizen that crossed the marines' path became subject to their approval. One mild afternoon in the Shia south, I accompanied a colonel making his rounds of the camp perimeter. We walked up to a sunburned sergeant sitting in a fighting hole with an M60 machine gun aimed at a Bedouin man praying on the sand a couple of hundred yards away.

The marine, never taking his eyes from the prostrate figure in flapping garments, told his commander, "As far as we can tell, he's not hostile, sir, and we're keepin' an eye on him to see if any unusual activity occurs."

The balding, pug-faced colonel responded paternally, "Marine, he considers this his tribal land, and he feels he has as much right to be out here as we do." Such was the logic of the invasion.

On the third day of the ground war, US forces ran into an enormous low-pressure system that extended from Saudi Arabia to Turkey. As the mighty *shamal* winds picked up, the air filled with blowing grit the consistency of talcum powder. The sky turned a ghostly orange, the color of unripened cantaloupe, and sand got into everything—laptops, sleeping bags, sound recorders, ears, eyes, underwear.

The violent sandstorm slowed the column to a crawl, but, being marines, they didn't stop. Disoriented trucks ran off the highway and rolled over in the soft sand. Our driver duct-taped her flashlight onto the rear of the Humvee trailer in front of her so she would have a beacon to follow. Amphibious assault tractors, called pigs because of their extended snoutlike fronts, passed us in the gloaming. Hour after hour, these lumbering things with shining eyes and screaming motors seemed like dinosaurs on a doomed, final trek. In back of the truck, we journalists lay about in flak vests with handkerchiefs tied over our faces and watched sand pour in through the flap. A caged pigeon named Skittles, one of dozens acquired by the marines as disposable sentinels to detect poisonous gas, keeled over dead, sandstruck.

Woozy from sleeplessness, I fantasized that the sandstorm was an omen, a supernatural curse unleashed by Allah to stop the infidel

American Crusaders with their *Maxim* magazines, Gameboys, and MRE Lorna Doones. Were we doomed?

After 27 hours of this, our truck wheezed to a halt. Like Kabuki actors rising from the grave, we sand-encrusted reporters climbed from our traveling compartment and stepped into the twilight. The shamal had intensified to a hurricane of sand. Breathing without a handkerchief was like inhaling coffee grounds. We formed a daisy chain and made our way into the chaplain's tent, wondering how much worse it would get. "At least we're not getting mortared," said Schweitzer, who later earned a Combat Action Ribbon for his service in the Iraq war.

I heard rumbling in the distance. Artillery? No, it was thunder. The sandstorm suddenly became a monsoon. Big raindrops soaked the sand, and water flowed under the tent flaps. We frantically bermed up the sides and pulled our gear into the middle to keep it dry. John Kifner, who'd been everywhere and covered everything in his 30 years with the *New York Times*, uttered two words: "peanut butter."

"It rained like this during Desert Storm when I was with the 101st in Saudi Arabia. The desert's going to turn into peanut butter," said Kifner, and he was right. When the rain stopped and we emerged from the chaplain's tent, we stepped into a world of cleansed light and curses about "goose shit."

But it was nothing compared to the night that Corporal Jason Lee had spent in his fighting hole a couple of hundred yards from us. The trumpeter/machine gunner spent hours in the howling sandstorm and then the deluge. "I can honestly say this was the worst day of my life," he told me, his face caked with grit. "It's a terrifying feeling to know the enemy could be a half mile away, and we couldn't see anything or hear anything. I just wanted to curl up and hope nothin' bad happened to me."

The grunts never knew exactly what to make of the reporters. They couldn't understand how we could enter a war zone without a weapon. In my only firefight, an ambush by a group of *Fedayeen* (Saddam loyalists) with terrible aim, I cowered in the back of a Humvee. The turret gunner kicked an M-16 in my lap and yelled, "You're from Texas—use that thing!" I declined and spared the USMC a friendly-fire incident.

All in all, though, the grunts didn't seem to mind having us along. I put them on the air so their spouses and sweethearts and mothers would know they were okay. I let them use my satellite phone to call home. They appreciated my shortwave radio because most grunts didn't know what the hell was going on in the war. Every evening they gathered around to listen to the BBC World Service and hear the latest quote from the Iraqi information minister, the unforgettable Mohammed Saeed al-Sahaf. "The American mercenaries are nowhere near the airport," he would say. "They are lost in the desert. . . . They cannot read a compass. . . . They are retarded." The grunts hooted and high-fived.

What the marines really liked was my colleague, Mercedes Gallego, a gutsy 32-year-old reporter for the Spanish daily *El Correo* who had wangled an embed slot from the Pentagon brass. Mercedes was a knockout even when she was coated in dust and hadn't bathed in weeks. Wherever she went in the batallion, she was a one-person USO show.

One day, she heard that the shock trauma platoon had rigged up a field shower—four hospital litters stood up to form a stall around a hanging water bag. They offered it to her, and she accepted. Mercedes stepped inside, and pieces of clothing began appearing over the tops of the cots. To this day, it's unclear whether the Cobra gunship that appeared directly overhead happened to be going to the landing zone or whether alert marines called in the chopper at the precise moment Mercedes began to soap her torso. Under the violent prop wash, the flimsy aluminum cots fluttered into the desert. For a flickering instant the sandstorms and bad food and bellowing gunnery sergeant didn't matter. The navy docs scrambled to get her a towel. Life mimicks cinema. Had someone remembered the similar scene in the movie *M*A*S*H* with Sally Kellerman as Hotlips Hoolihan?

"It seemed like an accident, but maybe I'm naive," Mercedes said later with a good-natured shrug. "All I know is I was upset because I couldn't wash my hair."

Day in and day out, the greatest challenge of traveling with the marines was finding a place to work. While the war machine slumbered in the Middle East, it was deadline eight hours earlier at NPR headquarters in Washington. Under the nighttime doctrine of "light discipline," we were under strict orders not to emit any light that might attract a sniper. How, then, to write my story on a laptop computer whose screen glowed like a campfire?

There was no good solution. If we were lucky, the colonel would kick the chaplain out of his light-insulated tent and let us use it. But that didn't happen often because a lot of grunts were coming to Jesus. One reporter tried zipping himself inside his sleeping bag, pecking away on the keyboard as he became soaked with sweat. One dark night, I invited myself into the back of a field ambulance to type my story before the doctor eventually chased me out. The big shots in the combat operations tent usually didn't want me around because I might see the battle map. With deadline approaching, I would sometimes boot up my Toshiba under the stars and damn the rules.

"Reporter, shut off that light before I shove it up your ass!" the gunnery sergeant bellowed. "You want to get your fucking grape shot?" "Grape" meaning "head" in marinespeak. Later, I loaned my sat phone

center of the Universe." The local chamber of commerce scrambled to turn lemons into lemonade. They set up a booth in the convention center and urged—actually begged—reporters to say something good about the city. They suggested visits to "A Taste of Waco," hosted by the Waco Restaurant Association; the Dr Pepper Museum; the miniature-horse show at the Heart O' Texas Fairgrounds; or a performance of *Romeo and Juliet* at the Baylor Theatre. But it was useless. The Branch Davidian siege was a public relations nightmare. The world was watching, and what it saw fit every stereotype of the Lone Star State.

"Dropped in the middle of the dusty Texas prairie," began a dispatch in the *London Times*, "the city of Waco is a place of pickup trucks and drive-ins, Stetsons, poverty, religious devotion, and lots of guns." The correspondent went on to report "fresh vegetables appear to be illegal," and reporters wear Hawaiian shirts "made out of a sort of refined plastic" from Wal-Mart, "Waco's nearest equivalent of a clothes shop."

Within the FBI encampment, brains were losing ground and testosterone was gaining. The Hostage Rescue Team was tired. They were concerned about a mass breakout with the kids used as human shields. They worried about a .50-caliber sniper rifle they spotted in the tower that had a range of 3,000 yards. They simply didn't believe Koresh would ever give up and lead his people out. They thought he was a con man using "Bible babble" to stall for time. The FBI noted in a postincident evaluation, "Koresh made no threats, set no deadlines, and made no demands." The tactical side wanted action.

In the final weeks of the standoff, reporters finally began to hear from a few alternative sources. Two crackerjack criminal lawyers from Houston, Dick DeGuerin and Jack Zimmerman, were permitted 20 hours of visits with Koresh and his followers. When they came out, they told us the Davidians wanted very much to come out but would do so only after Koresh finished decoding the secrets of the seven seals, which he indicated would take a couple more weeks. But Koresh had already broken two promises to come out, and the FBI saw his exposition of the seals as simply another delaying tactic.

Then two experts on apocalyptic religion emerged—James Tabor, of the University of North Carolina, and Phillip Arnold, of the Reunion Institute in Houston—who showed a keen understanding of what Koresh was saying about the book of Revelation. According to these men, Koresh was not spouting Bible babble; his interpretation had internal logic and consistency. They believed they could reason with Koresh because they could speak his language.

By this time it was too late. The waiting game was over. On the night of April 17, 48 days after the siege began, Attorney General Janet Reno secretly gave the go-ahead for the final assault.

I always had a bad feeling about this story. As the impasse wore on, winter turned to spring, and the pastures along FM Road 2491 erupted with bluebonnets, Indian paintbrush, wild snapdragons, and the welcome smell of spring. I was a gardener, so the season of things budding and flowering filled me with the pleasurable awareness of rebirth, not death. But then I would reach Satellite City, with its black lenses pointed northeast and the grim state troopers blocking traffic, and a creeping sensation of something dreadful and foreordained would return.

I was at home early on Monday, April 19, when I got the call from the NPR news desk: "Something's up at Waco. The AP is saying the FBI is assaulting the compound in tanks. You'd better get up there."

I jumped in the family Honda, raced the 100 miles north, and flew off the exit ramp. Driving out to the roadblock, I noticed wildflowers straining against an unseasonably blustery wind.

When I arrived, a friendly cameraman let me watch the TV monitor inside his van. What I saw was M-60 tanks mounted with gas-spewing booms methodically punching holes in the flimsy walls of the main building. Agents in Bradley Fighting Vehicles were launching hundreds of ferret tear-gas rounds into the building. Other Bradleys started breaching walls to create escape routes and open more spaces for tear-gas canisters. The Davidians opened fire, and the FBI escalated the gassing.

Agents hoped maternal instinct would take over, and mothers would whisk their babies out of the gassed buildings and walk out toward a Red Cross flag. That's not how it turned out. Ricks insisted, "This is not an assault" and "This is not an indication our patience has run out," which was wrong on both counts.

By noon, the gassing had gone on for six hours. The phone into the complex had gone dead, so all communication had ceased. A 25-mph wind was blowing the gas away so effectively that many of the Davidians inside never even donned their gas masks.

At 12:01 p.m., an FBI negotiator on a loudspeaker announced, "David, you have had your 15 minutes of fame. Vernon is no longer the Messiah. Leave the building now."

At about 12:10, standing at the barricade, I watched the first clouds of black smoke curl into the sky. In a matter of seconds, it seemed, bright orange flames were shooting from the windows. The usually boisterous, wisecracking press corps fell silent. Everyone was wondering the same thing—what about the children? They never had a chance to reject their father's doomsday philosophy.

Fanned by the wind, the flimsy plywood and two-by-four structure became a bonfire on the prairie. Fire trucks were held back out of fear the Davidians would shoot at them. At one point, follower Ruth Riddle jumped off the roof and tried to run back inside the burning building; an agent ran in and dragged her out as she tried to fight him off. FBI agents heard what they called systematic gunfire inside the buildings.

It was all over in less than 40 minutes, the buildings and everything inside them efficiently reduced to charcoal. Nine Davidians escaped, one wearing a black T-shirt with the words "David Koresh God Rocks." Seventy-four Davidians, including 21 children, died from asphyxiation, injuries from collapsing debris, and self-inflicted and consensual gunshots, an independent panel later determined.

Though the FBI controlled the information for 51 days, Koresh had the last say. Revelation 6:9: "And when he had opened the fifth seal, I saw under the altar the souls of them that were slain for the word of God, and for the testimony which they held."

In the years following the Waco debacle, widespread criticism fell on the FBI. Some believe allegations by surviving Davidians that the agents intentionally or accidentally started the fire at Mount Carmel. Others buy into the speculative accusations made in the documentary film *Waco: The Rules of Engagement* that FBI riflemen shot at fleeing Davidians. But one doesn't have to enter the realm of conspiracy to acknowledge that the agency committed tragic mistakes and terribly mismanaged the siege at Waco.

The gas attack, in its planning and execution, was a fiasco. Senator John McCain called it "an ill-conceived exercise of federal authority that led to the unnecessary loss of life."

Van Zandt, now a private security consultant after 25 years in the FBI, says, "The Davidians set the fire. Did the FBI pour psychological fuel on that fire? I think we did. Even though the Davidians lit the match, I think we were partly responsible. Because we didn't try everything we should have."

An internal investigation by the Department of Treasury, which oversees the ATF, concluded the February 28 assault was flawed from the beginning. The raid planners never should have made the decision to go forward once the element of surprise was lost. As a direct result, ATF director Stephen Higgins and five other high-ranking officials resigned, and the agency's image has still not recovered.

In 2000, seven years after the fire, former Senator John C. Danforth released an exhaustive independent investigation that largely exonerated the FBI. The report concluded that the government did not cause the fire; the Davidians spread Coleman lantern fuel throughout the main structure and started fires in at least three locations. Among the mountain of evidence, a Davidian held a sign outside a window several days before the fire with the message "The flames await: Isaiah 13."

The report further concluded that FBI agents did not shoot at Koresh's followers the morning of April 19. Pathology studies concluded that at least 20 Davidians were shot and one was stabbed, including 5 victims under age 14, in acts of suicide or consensual execution. The report concluded that an FBI agent recklessly shot three pyrotechnic military tear-gas rounds at a construction pit near the complex. While there is no evidence the pyrotechnic rounds started the fatal fire, the FBI lied about it for six years, covered up damning evidence, and stonewalled investigators. But in the end, the Danforth report laid the tragedy squarely at the feet of David Koresh and his closest followers.

What has haunted me since 1993 is whether we in the media, who are always so quick to assign blame, share a portion of the responsibility for the calamity at Waco.

"The atmosphere was, 'Finally, they're doing something.' The story had gotten expensive to cover, and a lot of people were pulling out. I remember the relief and delight a lot of reporters felt when the feds launched the assault. It's not a pretty picture to paint of ourselves," said Potok, who now works at the Southern Poverty Law Center.

The most common complaint against us is how we parroted the FBI's use of the loaded terms "compound" and "cult" without skepticism. Religion scholars believe the words militarized and demeaned a legitimate, though unconventional, millennial religious community. The constant reference to "the Davidian compound" carried military connotations and was inaccurate; a compound must be enclosed by a fence or wall, and Mount Carmel was open.

Use of the word "cult" is more complicated. According to the dictionary, a cult is a religion regarded as unorthodox or spurious, which, to me, accurately describes the Davidians, with their brainwashing, firearms arsenal, and child brides. But the word does carry negative overtones that played into the hands of police agencies.

Catherine Wessinger, professor of religious studies at Loyola University, New Orleans, charges in her book *How the Millennium Comes Violently: From Jonestown to Heaven's Gate* that the media "dehumanized" the Davidians. "The media coverage produced a cultural consensus that their deaths did not warrant public outcry against the excessive force used against them." She concluded that "reporters in search of sensationalized stories of conflict contributed to the tragic conclusions."

My colleague Wade Goodwyn, for whom the Branch Davidians was his first big story for NPR, shares my concern. "When I got there, David Koresh was a redneck, rock-and-roll hick who thought he was Jesus. That's what we wrote. That's how the FBI talked about it. I felt responsible for demonizing the cult. It left a bitter taste in my mouth, one that never went away," he said.

No institution spins like the US government. Reporters are, on the whole, too willing to accept Washington's enemy du jour, whether

Manuel Noriega of Panama, Saddam Hussein of Baghdad, or David Koresh of Waco. This doesn't mean they aren't bad guys. It means that the media is being used by the government, in all likelihood, to prepare the public for a hostile action against these enemies of the state. Journalists, like screenwriters, have a tendency to look for a story line, for simplified drama, for conventional wisdom. We're blackbirds in search of the same wire.

Three weeks after the fire, I got my first glimpse of the Davidians as real people. I had asked two surviving Davidian women if we might visit the group's original home near Palestine, Texas, where the Davidians had lived in the mid-1980s before moving to Mount Carmel.

The women and I drove together from Waco in my minivan in awkward silence, them not trusting me and me wondering if they were kooks. We pulled onto a road of red clay and threaded our way through slash pine to a rustic encampment of plywood shacks. About 80 followers had lived out there, shivering in winter and sweating in summer, hauling water, using outhouses, and studying Isaiah and Malachi by the light of kerosene lanterns. They had accepted this life of reclusiveness and privation to be close to the young Vernon Howell before he became David Koresh.

My guides were Janet Kendrick, the gray-haired caretaker of the property, and Janet McBean, a Jamaica-born nurse who'd been living in California when the trouble erupted in Waco. They were gentle, pious women who tried to help me understand what they believed. I wished I had met them earlier.

"What's going to happen in the future is so wonderful for us," Kendrick said. "We have promises from the Bible of things to come. Our friends who died, we'll see them again. They've just gone on ahead of us."

As we walked through the settlement, I realized I could have been talking to adherents of any denomination who espoused a fairly standard belief in heaven and eternal life. Yet there was something troubling about the lack of emotion the two Janets displayed when they talked about the terrible immolation deaths of so many friends and innocent children. McBean's own brother, Wayne Martin, had died in the fire, along with two of his children. Even a profound belief in an afterlife, I thought, doesn't negate grief.

"I hope he didn't suffer," she said matter-of-factly in her Caribbean-accented English. "When I saw the fire, I knew God wanted it this way. My brother's spirit has gone up to wherever it needs to go right now so he can be resurrected with a new body and so on."

I asked about Koresh's kids. McBean hesitated. "There's something special about those children that the world doesn't know," she said.

"This whole fiasco happened because of the children, okay? The seven seals talk about those children. People believed in the seven seals because of those children. We didn't know how those children were going to return to heaven."

Kendrick again: "We were never told exactly how it would happen. God didn't ever draw up a plan, okay? We just knew something was going to happen, but we did not know what."

We all three stood in a clearing of pine trees, the warm spring sunlight mottling the ground and bringing out the sharp aroma of pine needles. The urgency in their voices and the seriousness in their faces indicated that we had finally arrived. This is what they believed.

McBean again: "It all has to do with judgment, because there's going to be a judgment. You are going to turn to God, and you are going to say, 'God, I do not deserve the punishment that you are going to give me. I never heard of David Koresh. I never knew about the seven seals.' "

I realized that she was now talking directly at me.

"And God is going to say, 'That's not true, John. You attended those news conferences in Waco, and you took the FBI's word as gospel and did not go and search it out for yourself.' "

So that was it. The journalists covering the Branch Davidian standoff not only got snookered by the FBI but had a front-row seat to prophecy, and we blew it. We squandered our chance at immortality. For us unbelievers, there would be a special punishment—earthquakes, plagues, locusts, and an eternal press conference presided over by a blonde police sergeant with lion's teeth and the tale of a scorpion, who tormented reporters with the phrase "One question and a follow-up, no shouting, if you shout you will be ignored" until we longed for death.

Chapter 4

GUATEMALA:
CLUB SANDWICH OF FEAR

THE GUATEMALAN COUP D'ÉTAT of August 8, 1983, followed the time-honored script of Central American military rebellions. In a show of force, a pair of Cessna Dragonflies from the Guatemalan air force droned back and forth over the National Palace, an ornate green fortress the color of the American dollar. Radio stations played the national anthem. The *golpistas*, the army faction intent on overthrowing the government, turned their khaki military shirts inside out so as not to be confused with the soldiers defending the palace. It was shirts versus skins, Guatemala style.

The day of the *golpe de estado*—literally, the "blow to the state"— was my first day as the new Guatemala stringer for United Press International, or "la Upi," as it was known throughout Latin America. Fresh out of Spanish language school, I was as green as the besieged palace. I grabbed my notebook and trotted the five blocks to the park, past the central market with its displays of psychedelic purple fruit and the flyswatter seller who chanted *"matamoscas, matamoscas"* all day. Gleeful boys passed me, sprinting toward the palace like fans to a soccer celebration, because in Central America, a *golpe* is the best free entertainment in town.

When I arrived, panting, the park was surrounded by soldiers pointing their automatic weapons at the palace while armored personnel carriers idled at intersections. Throughout downtown, I heard *slam*, *slam*, *slam* as shopkeepers pulled down metal shutters to protect their businesses amid the bedlam. A breathless young officer rushed out of the palace's massive wooden doors, stood on a park bench, and started speaking. I scribbled down what I could understand: "The legitimate government of the republic is fighting against a coup by corrupt commanders. . . ."

I pressed a quetzal, the national currency, into the hand of a motorcyclist and asked for a lift back to the office. The army had severed all phone service, making it impossible for me to send my first alert to Mexico City. *Ay dios.* Coups are always a huge story. Alert bells were ringing on teletypes from Ontario to Buenos Aires. I was an eyewitness to history, and I couldn't get through to my editor.

I ran back to the park, sweat staining my new khaki suit, and stood with a clutch of local journalists off to one side of the square. A portly, kinky-haired reporter for *El Gráfico* named Jorge was explaining to me the nuances of interarmy politics when the shooting started. In a blur of cheap suits and bouncing bellies, the journalists scattered down Eighth Avenue. Behind us, assault rifles burped back and forth between aggressors and loyalists. Jorge and I dove behind a parked car. A candle seller in front of the Catedral Nacional shrieked, crossed herself, and crawled under her stand, spilling *Nuestro Redentor* prayer cards on the sidewalk.

When the shooting stopped, I dashed into the open door of El Colegio de los Infantes, a private Catholic school attached to the cathedral. Inside, nuns were trying to calm the whimpering students in their blue-and-white school uniforms. From the doorway, I watched as a heavyset woman with a large shopping bag carefully stepped over a soldier in a prone position, then glanced back with a maternal, boys-will-be-boys look and hurried on to the bus stop.

The coup was the beginning of two turbulent years I spent in Guatemala that taught me about life, death, love, and corruption. That's where it all happened. I formed a lifelong attachment to this meso-American nation the size of Tennessee, with its extremes of poverty and wealth, fog-shrouded volcanoes, ancient Mayan faces, and curse of violence. Guatemala is where I got my start in radio. And Guatemala is where I met Ginny, who became my wife.

I had chosen the country quite by chance. Working as a reporter at the *San Antonio Express-News* had aroused my interest in learning Spanish and understanding Latin America. In the summer of 1983, I quit my job, sold all my furniture, left my girlfriend, and moved south to the old colonial capital of Antigua to enroll in Spanish language school. The laid-back, cobblestoned city was a welcome refuge from the guerrilla war that was convulsing the country.

Antigua possessed an aphrodisiac power. Perhaps it was the constant threat of earthquakes or the collective pollen of so many tropical gardens or the bygone murmur of confessions lingering over the ruins of so many crumbled churches. One afternoon, I found myself touring a former indigo plantation, said to be haunted by blue ghosts, that was the summer residence of a group of graduate students from Tulane University. My guide, Virginia Garrard, was a tall, good-looking, olive-eyed Texan, the daughter of an Episcopal priest from Sherman, only an hour away from my hometown of Dallas. We started dating.

I had planned to freelance for a few months in Guatemala until my money ran out, then head back to Texas newspapering. But I learned that UPI was looking for a Guatemala City stringer. With only a basic grasp of conversational Spanish, I called up the regional editor in Mexico City and talked my way into the job. Ginny returned to New Orleans in the fall, and I moved to Guatemala City to become a wire-service reporter.

The UPI office was located inside the building of the oldest newspaper in the country, *El Imparcial*. Contrary to its name, the *Impartial* was the government's mouthpiece, the oligarch's defender, and the army's lapdog. The stringer I replaced was a senior reporter who embodied all these qualities.

Raul was a slim, suave mestizo with a pencil-thin mustache and was known for his friends in the palace and in the bedroom. At UPI in Mexico City, the Rolodex listed three numbers for Raul: office, home, and *casa chica*, or "girlfriend's house." His lover was a buck-toothed, heavily perfumed *Imparcial* secretary named Ofelia, who brought him a glass of milk for his ulcer every afternoon and granted him exclusive access to her tectonic cleavage. After the *golpe*, the new military head of state tapped Raul to be Guatemala's ambassador to Panama, and, thankfully, we never heard from him again.

Every time I walked up the ink-smeared steps into *El Imparcial*, I felt I was entering a movie set for a Latin remake of *The Front Page*. Reporters wore dark suits, white shirts, and skinny black ties. They worked on manual Smith Coronas, cigarettes smoldering in ashtrays and bottles of Venado rum stashed in file cabinets. They were all *faferos*, underpaid journalists who took payoffs from news sources, and they always resented me as the gringo interloper who had unseated Raul. I never trusted them. One *Imparcial* reporter who worked part-time for UPI was paid by army intelligence to keep track of my whereabouts.

Nothing ever changed at *El Imparcial*. On the day of the coup, the biggest story all year, the portly old editor in chief looked up at the clock at 5:30 p.m., collected his briefcase, and imperturbably walked out of the newsroom. Governments came and governments went.

Guatemala never seemed to change either. I was witnessing the Guatemalan military purging itself, which it did periodically. The outgoing president, retired general José Efraín Ríos Montt, was replaced by the defense minister, a stout, 53-year-old brigadier general named Oscar Humberto Mejía Victores. He was a career officer who could be counted on to caretake the republic and leave *la institución armada* alone to do what it did best: feather its nest and destroy its enemies. After six months under the new chief of state, a Canadian diplomat I knew began referring to him as "the neanderthal."

Ríos Montt, who had seized power in a coup 18 months earlier, was an oddball even by the eccentric standards of Latin American potentates. His mustache was prematurely white, which made him look like a figure in a "Got Milk?" ad. He was a born-again evangelical Christian who went on national television each Sunday night to preach temperance, morality, and redemption, and he called on God to heal his benighted nation. He conned everybody. At one point, he appeared on *The 700 Club*, where host Pat Robertson implored his viewers to "pray around the clock for Ríos Montt."

In the course of his crusade to create la Nueva Guatemala, Ríos Montt estranged the same army that had granted him power. The military tired of his erratic style and theocratic streak. He had committed the unpardonable sin of promoting young officers over the heads of the old-line generals who were accustomed to running the nation like a board of directors. No one in the military, however, could fault Ríos Montt for his antiguerrilla strategy.

The August coup was a sideshow to the larger story of the ongoing insurgency, then 23 years old. We know now it was the most savage of Central America's armed conflicts. More people were killed in Guatemala's counterinsurgency war than in Nicaragua, El Salvador, and Honduras combined. While Ríos Montt told Bible stories on TV, his troops were conducting a savage scorched-earth campaign in the Maya highlands, where the guerrillas were active. The worst of the slaughter ended the year before I arrived. From 1981 to 1983, security forces machine-gunned, hacked, bludgeoned, choked, and burned alive an estimated 20,000 people and erased 440 Mayan villages from the map according to the International Center for Human Rights Research. The butchery peaked in April 1982 with 3,330 victims, or 111 a day—a death every 15 minutes.

The targets were guerrillas and virtually anyone who worked for social change. In the countryside, that meant catechists, priests, health promoters, social workers, even teachers. In the cities, it was leftist politicians, trade unionists, university students, lawyers, journalists, professors, and human rights activists. As the colonels liked to say, the armed forces were draining the sea in which the fish—the guerrillas—swam.

The Carter administration had instituted a ban on US military aid to Guatemala because of gross human rights violations, but the Israeli government happily stepped in to sell the armed forces everything from war planes to assault rifles. Other US allies in the region watched Guatemala with admiration. I once asked a Salvadoran army colonel how his country would fight its insurgency differently if the US embassy weren't watching so closely. With a cobra's smile, he answered, "We would employ the Guatemalan solution."

The best description I ever heard of life in Guatemala came from my onetime landlady, a German widow who spent her days listening to Verdi and drinking Kirschwasser. "The sergeants are afraid of the captains, the foot soldiers are afraid of the sergeants, and the Indians are afraid of them all," she said. "Guatemala is a club sandwich of fear."

As a 27-year-old journalist trying to make sense of the madness, my rudimentary vocabulary expanded into areas not covered by my Spanish grammar workbook: *el machetazo*, "the machete wound"; *el tiroteo*, "the gunfight"; *el feretro*, "the coffin"; *desaparecer*, "to disappear";

emboscar, "to ambush"; *ametrallado*, "shot with a machine gun"; and the national invective, *hijos de la gran puta!* or "sons of the great whore!"

The ascendance of Mejia Victores signaled the evolution of the counterinsurgency strategy. With the Marxist guerrillas on the run, the mass murder of Mayans and the decimation of their villages became increasingly unnecessary. The next phase, the one I witnessed, would be the consolidation phase—what the army called civic action. The military herded displaced Indians into newly constructed, army-controlled camps euphemistically called model villages. Tens of thousands of men were forced into antiguerrilla militias called civilian self-defense patrols, which began to commit their own atrocities. Yet there was much mopping up to be done. The death squads still had long lists of real and imagined collaborators in the cities and countryside. In order to keep the sea drained, the Guatemalan state continued to use the strategic application of terror.

This was the backdrop for my growing romance with Ginny. She had moved from New Orleans to Guatemala City to continue the field research for her dissertation about the growth of Protestantism in Guatemala. I tagged along with her when she visited a tiny Prince of Peace church in Chimaltenango Province to interview the pastor. She followed me to Chiquimula when I reported on the miraculous sighting of the image of the virgin that appeared in a wasp's nest. Our idea of a date was to park at the *trébol*, a cloverleaf intersection in Guatemala City where you could buy *taquitos* and bottles of Gallo beer and hire mariachis to serenade you.

From the beginning, we shared the same skewed appreciation of Guatemala. We looked forward to Holy Week, when young men went door-to-door, demanding tips to beat up a dummy of Judas. We loved the marimba for its disconnect between the gay, carnival-sounding music and the sad, stoic musicians in their matching leisure suits. We were constantly on the lookout for the national topiary—bushes trimmed into the shape of the national bird, the quetzal. And we scanned newspapers for only-in-Guatemala oddities, such as the photograph of the surgeon holding up an enormous tumor he'd removed, like a Georgia farmer showing off a prizewinning pumpkin.

As the months passed and I grew into the job at UPI, it became apparent that Guatemala was the most overlooked story in Central America. US correspondents would parachute in for a few days but couldn't wait to get back to San Salvador, Managua, Tegucigalpa, or Miami. "I could never live here; it's too creepy," a *New York Times* reporter told me on her way out of town.

They also understood that there was a limited news hole for stories about Guatemala. It's a sad reality of American journalism that the US State Department unofficially sets the agenda for most foreign-assignment editors. Under President Ronald Reagan's view of Central America, only two conflicts mattered: El Salvador, where the administration was spending as much as $1.5 million a day to defeat the FMLN (Farabundo Marti National Liberation Front) rebels; and Nicaragua, where the administration was bankrolling the contras to topple Nicaragua's leftist Sandinistas. As the regional correspondent for Reuters once told me airily, "Guatemala is just not the story."

But it was my story.

Journalists never understood the full dimensions of the carnage in Guatemala, partly because the conflict was so maddeningly difficult to report on. In El Salvador, reporters could tape "TV" onto the windows of their taxis, drive into the mountains to visit guerrilla-held territory, and be back in the hotel bar for *cuba libres* after deadline. Or they could tune in to rebel radio and hear what happened that day in the war. Guatemala's four leftist guerrilla groups, who called themselves the Guatemalan National Revolutionary Unity, rarely engaged in major battles, rarely held formally "liberated" territory, and rarely took journalists with them into the bush.

The Guatemalan army was no easier to cover. As an institution, it was xenophobic, fanatically proud, and hermetic; "a samurai brotherhood," a longtime lawyer in the capital told me. The generals disliked foreign correspondents in particular. They considered us de facto subversives because our stories portrayed Guatemala in a negative light and hurt investment and tourism. The military even had a term for it: *desprestigiar la patria*, "to damage the prestige of the fatherland."

One day I was summoned to the office of the chief army spokesman, Edgar Djalma Dominguez, a trim infantry colonel with a resonant voice like a radio announcer. He wanted to complain to me about a story in *Time* magazine in which I had shared a byline. When I sat down before his desk, I expected him to take issue with the large number of kidnappings and disappearances we had attributed to the Guatemalan security forces. But I was wrong. He was upset about an adjective the lead writer had used to describe General Mejia. "How dare you refer to the chief of state as 'paunchy'!" Djalma boomed.

I learned an important lesson that day. You can call a Latin American strongman a murderer; just don't slight his vanity.

One of the challenges of working in Guatemala was my height. Journalism textbooks say to be unobtrusive, a "fly on the wall." This works fine when a reporter is covering the Texas legislature, but it simply doesn't apply to someone six-foot-seven in the land of the Maya.

One day at the palace, some painters left a ladder in the corridor, and a particularly squat TV reporter climbed up on the second rung to have a chat with me. Everyone yukked it up, and a photographer for *Prensa Libre* snapped a picture. I assumed the photo would end up on the newspaper's bulletin board. The next day, the photo ran under the cutline "Journalists of Height" on the front page of the most widely read newspaper in the country.

I had become a national freak. A couple of weeks after the *Prensa Libre* shot, I boarded a public bus, and a woman leaned toward her friend and pointed her finger. I heard her whisper, "That's him."

It became a liability when I traveled to Maya villages to research army atrocities. I intended to arrive quietly and conduct my interviews discreetly, but my visit caused a commotion comparable to the arrival of a circus parade. Gaggles of children followed me down the street, daring one another to dash up and touch the Enormous Gringo. Strangers approached me on the street to ask my shoe size. Once, in Santa Cruz del Quiche, a teacher let her entire class out to come and view me, as though I were homework for a kinesiology lesson.

During the first year of my Guatemalan sojourn, I heard a report of a skirmish between the army and ORPA, the Revolutionary Organization of Armed People, in an upland coffee plantation of San Marcos Province on the country's Pacific slope. The rebels had been operating in the coffee belt for years, organizing peasants, burning farm buildings, and hijacking payrolls. Unfamiliar with that part of the country, I wanted to find out why the insurgents targeted farmworkers.

My traveling partner was Anson Ng, the British-educated son of a Malaysian rubber baron who had rejected the lucrative family business and made his way to Central America to become a journalist. Anson was even greener than I was, but there were so few foreign reporters in Guatemala in those days that we teamed up. We took the coastal highway through a series of decaying villages whose economies revolved around the speed bumps that slowed traffic enough to provide business for the ambulatory coconut vendors, cigarette sellers, and big-hipped *putas*. Then we turned northeast and began the slow climb into the mountains that form a volcanic ridge running from central Mexico south to Panama. On these slopes grows some of the most savory arabica coffee in the Americas, and the seasonal workers who pick the beans are among the most wretched migrants in the hemisphere.

When we finally arrived at Finca Concepción Candelaria, the living quarters looked like a concentration camp. Men slept in bunks in decrepit wood and bamboo barracks with dirt floors and no latrines or running water. Children ran around with bare, scabrous bottoms and wracking coughs. They were Jacaltec Mayas from neighboring Huehuetenango Province, a focus of army counterinsurgency sweeps. The intricate and colorful embroidery on their clothes was the same image used in national tourism campaigns to promote travel to this happy and carefree country. But the workers' clothing was little more than a matrix of patches, the brilliant colors worn to dullness.

The men earned $2 a day working the coffee harvest from dawn to dusk—half the national minimum wage. From this, the administrator deducted the workers' advances, their bus fare to and from the finca, and the corn and beans that made up their diet. The pay and living conditions were deplorable, but the Indians had few options. Back in their home villages, their small plots of corn were only productive during the rainy season, so they were forced to find seasonal work to provide for their families.

That was my epiphany. I had never until that moment understood how poverty can fuel rebellion. As a Texas-based reporter, I'd been to the *colonias* in border counties where shyster developers sold Mexicans plots of land lacking water and paved roads. But nothing prepared me for the living conditions of these 1,500 workers in San Marcos.

The workers told me a band of ORPA rebels had stayed with the coffee pickers for two nights and lectured them about exploitation and workers' rights. An army informant in the camp had squealed. On the second day, a military helicopter had swooped down, firing on the guerrillas from the air. The rebels fired back before melting into the forest. No guerrillas or soldiers died in the fight, but four coffee pickers and a seven-year-old boy were killed in the crossfire.

The firefight interrupted the harvest and scattered the workers. Bags of beans spilled. A day of work had been lost. The army came and interrogated them all and lectured them about the lies and disorder spread by *los subversivos*. The Indians had buried their dead and gone back to work among the coffee trees that studded the green slopes that overlook the shimmering Pacific.

"Our lives are not easy. After the harvest, we are left with a few quetzales to bring back to our families," a 29-year-old picker named José Angel told me. "We just work. We know nothing of politics."

The next day Anson and I drove into the Cuchumatanes Mountains to see what conditions were like in Angel's home village. The lowlands smelled thickly of moisture and rot, and when we rose into the forested slopes, the air became sharp with pine sap and cooking fires. Miles after the end of the asphalt road, we reached a hamlet named San Miguel that was dominated by a machine gun behind a parapet of sandbags. A stern army lieutenant told us we would not be permitted to drive any farther because there was fighting ahead in the mountains. He refused an interview and demanded to see our passports. The Jacaltecs who passed us looked at us with drawn faces and terror in their eyes. Whatever had happened here had traumatized the town.

As soon as we left the lieutenant, we slipped into the hospital and tried to interview a woman visiting her son, who was recovering from a machete wound to his neck. I sat next to her on a bench and began speaking to her softly. Just as she started to come around, Anson pulled out a big microphone and shoved it in her face. She scurried away down the corridor.

I finally found a French doctor working for a humanitarian relief group and asked him what was going on. In a low, urgent voice, he said, "Terrible things have happened here. I cannot talk to you. We are being watched. You are putting everyone you speak to in danger. You should leave."

He was right, so we left. The town, including the hospital, was riddled with *orejas*, the "ears of the military." Every person we spoke to would be called before the lieutenant and interrogated as to what we had asked and what they had told us. We were imperiling everyone we interviewed. That's what it was like covering Guatemala.

A glimpse of the kinds of atrocities being committed in the area of San Miguel emerged years later in the Catholic Church's exhaustive Interdiocesan Project of the Recuperation of Historic Memory. This account came from an unnamed male, Case 1125, Huehuetenango, 1983. "They captured me and took me to the military base in Huehue-tenango. It was a sad time. They kept me there for 10 days, torturing me with my hands tied behind. I was so swollen I wished they had killed me. I saw the other poor torture victims—the mothers with their children. The children were kept on one side, and the women were taken to a room where they were raped in front of the other women, [the soldiers behaving] like animals without respect. They did this in the day, and at midnight they killed them. I saw how they grabbed their heads and cut their throats. Then they put the bodies in a truck, and I don't know where they took them."

My adopted neighborhood was Zone One, the old commercial heart of the capital, whose habitués were characters in an endless street theater.

The blind lottery seller sat on a stool and cocked her ear for customers. It was considered good luck to buy a lottery ticket from a blind person. When footsteps approached, she shook her books of tickets and called out, "Win a new life!" On occasion, a boy no older than seven, zonked from sniffing glue, lay barebacked on a bed of broken beer bottles while his partner, a pock-faced man in mirrored sunglasses, hustled tips. On Sundays, young Indian housemaids took the day off and promenaded arm in arm along Sexta Avenida, teetering on clunky high heels and wearing the current fashion statement—a white slip protruding two inches below a dark skirt. Vendors peddled roasted corn with lime, mango slices with chili powder, and hot dogs squirted with sweet ketchup. Down at the *catedral*, beggars hauled themselves into the plaza to wait for the conclusion of morning mass so they could show off their ghastly wounds and misshapen limbs, twist their faces in pathos, and beg alms from the exiting worshippers. Across the park, yawning *taxistas* rubbed their tumid bellies and waited for a fare.

In the mornings, homeless people left piles of shit in the middle of the sidewalk, the caramel-colored dung always soft from bad diets, never firm from a steak dinner. In the evenings when I walked back from UPI, the pavement would be smeared and smelly. That was in the dry season. During the rainy season, warm cloudbursts came every afternoon to wash the sidewalks and purify the air, and for a little while before the darkness came, the city seemed clean and good again.

My apartment was on the top floor of the Hotel Mansion San Francisco, where a nightly symphony floated up the air shaft. A sawmill salesman expectorated; a husband raved and a wife wept; a prostitute moaned in practiced ecstasy; and in the ground-floor cantina, Pepsi mixed with *aguardiente* released men's souls, and they gripped the bar and emitted falsetto shouts that seemed to shift from rapture to grief and back again.

Days were eerily calm in the Guatemalan capital, and nights were terrifying. Violent death seemed to lurk just beyond the corona of the streetlights, at the edge of the city in the dark pine forests where the beings lived that inhabited the nightmares of children. One night Ginny and I walked out of a restaurant and watched a paneled van with darkened windows racing down Avenida la Reforma, running stoplights, with full knowledge of the hell in store for the captive within. Police interrogators extracted information with beatings, electric shocks, and more idiosyncratic methods: fiery chile sauce pumped up the nose, a face immersed to the point of drowning in toilet water, a plastic sack placed over the victim's head and sprayed full of pesticide.

The bodies were discovered in the morning floating in lakes, dumped along roadsides, or pitched in deep ravines called *barrancas* that surround the capital. They were hauled to the morgue by the popular firemen known as *los bomberos*, who seemed never to fight fires but only to collect cadavers. The *bomberos* always carried cameras with them to sell corpse shots to the scandal sheet *Extra!,* which published them on the cover: the philosophy professor with a bullet hole in his eye, the human rights advocate with his tongue torn out, the Christian Democrat with a wooden stake through his chest. *Extra!* always sold well.

At some point I picked up *El Señor Presidente*, the Nobel Prize–winning novel by Guatemalan author Miguel Ángel Asturias. Though it fictitiously describes the dictatorship of Manuel José Estrada Cabrera from 1898 to 1920, at the time it seemed uncannily relevant to my reality. "The weight of the dead makes the earth turn by night, and by day it is the weight of the living," he wrote. "When there are more dead than living there will be eternal night, night without end, for the living will not be heavy enough to bring the dawn."

And where was the Guatemalan press? By the time I arrived, 42 Guatemalan journalists had been kidnapped or murdered, according to the Association of Guatemalan Journalists in Exile, and the media had muzzled itself. There were no newsweeklies, signed editorials, or exposés; no muckraking deeper than "Insufficient Fire Hydrants in the Capital."

Death itself had lost its news value. I was in the palace one morning fishing for a juicy coup rumor, and I asked a *Prensa Libre* reporter what was going on. *"Solo los muertocitos,"* he said with a shrug. "Only the little deaths."

One night, Guatemala's popular TV news program, *Aquí El Mundo* (nicknamed "Aquí La Muerte"), ended its 10 o'clock broadcast with a ghoulish report about the discovery of a severed hand in a garbage pile. The camera showed a *bombero* holding up a coat hanger, and on the end of it dangled what looked like a shriveled brown glove. The stentorian announcer concluded his report, "The authorities are searching for the owner of the hand."

But everyone knew the authorities never searched for anything in Guatemala. The authorities existed only to show the world that the country had authorities. They never solved crimes, because if they did, everyone would know where the trail led, and that was the riddle implicit in the Big Lie. No group ever took credit for the corpses, and no nameable person was ever accused of murder. In Guatemala, violence seemed to happen like a natural calamity, like the 1976 earthquake.

My parents were scared to death that I was in Guatemala. My father, John, who owned a small advertising agency in Dallas, thought I was crazy for giving up a perfectly good newspaper job in San Antonio and moving to a country whose name he confused with "guacamole." My mother, Mary Helen, a Dallas socialite who tutored children with dyslexia, at least understood on some level that I wanted to explore the world. But she never stopped worrying about me. "Johnny," she said in our weekly phone calls, "you're not going into the countryside again, are you?"

What I didn't tell my mother was that danger was part of the allure of being in Guatemala—the adrenaline buzz of being in the vortex of a big, complicated, risky story. Plus, it was exotic. You never knew who you'd meet.

One of the American expats who drifted into Guatemala City in those days looking for adventure and cheap whores was Barry Sadler, the storied Vietnam veteran who wrote the 1966 hit "The Ballad of the Green Berets." We became drinking buddies in a downtown bar called the Europa, which served a delicious rabbit stew. Like so many mercenaries and wannabe mercs, Sadler had come to Central America during the 1980s. He was 44 when I met him and still built like the Special Forces sergeant he'd been. He never talked much about his entertainment career back in the sixties as a one-hit songwriter or his small parts in TV shows like *The High Chaparral*. By the time I met Barry, he was an arms dealer, a correspondent for *Soldier of Fortune* magazine, and the author of pulp fiction.

He had written a paperback series called "Casca: The Eternal Mercenary," about a centurion who spears Jesus on the cross and is cursed to fight throughout history as a reincarnated warrior, such as a samurai, a Mongol, a conquistador, and a French legionnaire. The fast-paced prose was masculine and violent, and Guatemala must have been an inspiration to his muse. "The streets were spattered with a rain of blood and meat and guts and spent lead. . . ." The 24 Casca novels have acquired a cult following and Barry Sadler the status of a folk hero.

My other drinking buddy at the Europa was Peter Wolfe, a bighearted, 27-year-old Peace Corps volunteer from Belmont, Michigan, who was helping Guatemalan conservation organizations. The work was apolitical and so was Peter. He looked so much like me—tall, lanky, glasses, goofy smile—that people used to confuse us. I once gave him a UPI business card and wrote "I'm not . . ." over my name and told him to present it the next time someone got us mixed up.

On October 27, 1984, I invited Peter to a birthday party for Ginny at my new apartment in Zone Two that overlooked a checkerboard of cornfields on a steep hillside. That night, we drank Botran rum with Coke, danced to cumbia, and tried to forget all about the *muertocitos*. After midnight, Peter said good-bye and set off on foot for his apartment about seven blocks away.

They discovered his body the next morning at first light. He was propped against a wall in the middle-class neighborhood where he lived, the entrance wound of a .38-caliber bullet in his left cheek. Theories flew in every direction. Robbery was ruled out when Peter's pocket watch turned up along with a wallet full of money. There were unsubstantiated rumors of a love triangle gone awry. Then there was the possibility of mistaken identity. I never seriously believed that the bullet was meant for me, but the rumor took off, and soon I got a frantic call from a friend in Managua urging me to leave the country.

I decided to resolve the second-guessing. I called a Guatemalan-born American named Harris Whitbeck who'd been a top adviser to Ríos Montt and was said to have excellent army contacts. Ginny and I went to his apartment and sat on his sofa while he poured me a glass of Johnny Walker.

"I need to know if my name is on a death list," I said.

"Let me make a phone call," Whitbeck responded, then walked into his bedroom and shut the door. He returned a few minutes later and said simply, "You're not on any list." That night we left his apartment so relieved, it was the next day before the journalist in me began to wonder who he called.

By this time the police, under pressure from the US embassy, had actually begun an investigation. Within a week of the murder, the newspapers carried a story about the arrest of a husky, 24-year-old thug named Boris René Acosta Días who lived in Peter's neighborhood. Peter's older brother, John Wolfe, a structural engineer in Berkeley, traveled to Guatemala to investigate the homicide. He learned that Acosta's public confession on television was forced by the brutal torture of his mother. He also learned that Acosta's family allegedly had judicial connections, and within weeks his file was "lost," and Acosta was released. He died in a motorcycle accident three years later.

"Boris was said to have a grudge against *norteamericanos*, and he and his friends were known to hang out in front of a store that Peter probably passed that night on his way home from your apartment," John Wolfe said. He concluded the homicide was not political and that Peter, in all likelihood, was in the wrong place at the wrong time.

Ginny and I were deeply shaken by Peter's murder, and we clung together in fear and love. It had finally shattered the anonymity of violent death in that country. The victim was no longer an expressionless face in the newspaper. My friend Julio Godoy, a Guatemalan journalist, told me gently, "Now you know what we feel."

When I arrived in Guatemala, there was not a single functioning human rights group left in the country. They had been wiped out or driven into exile. But in the spring of 1984, a new organization came into being that called itself the Mutual Support Group for the Appearance of Our Relatives Alive, known by its Spanish acronym, GAM.

GAM was formed by mostly middle-class women who had run into each other at the morgue, looking for the bodies of missing loved ones. Up to this time, a woman who pressed the authorities for the whereabouts of her disappeared husband was either ignored or suffered the same fate. From the beginning, however, the women of GAM correctly figured that they would be too loud to ignore and too numerous to send the death squads after. In the climate of fear and intimidation in which the security forces flourished, GAM did the unthinkable. They banged pots in the streets and tied up traffic; they invaded the national congress and blew whistles; they held placards bearing the pictures of disappeared loved ones and chanted, "Alive they were taken! Alive we want them back!"

The government didn't know what to do. The army invoked the Big Lie, claiming the missing were all subversives and had run off to fight in the mountains or train in Cuba. Mejía Victores publicly declared the women "a front for the subversives," and privately his colonels called them whores.

Death threats were delivered and made good on. Two members of GAM's steering committee, Hector Gomez Calito and Rosario Godoy de Cuevas, were murdered and their bodies mutilated.

Finally, when it was clear that GAM was not going away, Mejía Victores granted them an unprecedented audience. He received them in the Hall of Mirrors, a large hall of dark wood and ornately framed mirrors whose name evinces the warped reality that transpired there. The women of GAM stood awkwardly next to floor-to-ceiling drapes decorated with gold thread. I stood off to the side with the usual contingent of *caza-noticias*, "newshounds."

"Mr. Chief of State," began a plaintive woman in a plaid shirt and thick glasses, speaking into a microphone, "it is very powerful to have a husband taken. For nine months my son asks if his papa is dead. It is a terrible situation we are living. We have gone to the police, to the interior ministry, to the military base, to the morgue, but there is nothing."

Mejía Victores, his bulldog face expressionless, sat in a high-backed episcopal chair and smoked while they spoke. Only the tapping of his shiny military shoe betrayed his discomfort.

"You have in your hands so many disappeared, Mr. Chief of State," she continued. "I speak to your heart. Send them to the tribunals—do something. We have a pain that is so great."

The women wept. One after another they stood and spoke to the general, who watched them and smoked and tapped his foot.

A bronze-skinned Kakchiquel Indian woman wearing a traditional embroidered blouse and cradling a tiny suckling baby in her rebozo walked up to the microphone. It was rare for a Mayan to get an audience with the godlike head of state and rarer still to speak of political disappearances. I expected her voice to be a whisper.

"My husband was tortured by elements of the security forces. We have proof of this," she began, and the entire room inhaled. "I know the guerrillas did not kidnap him as the authorities told us. Virgilio was taken from the market where he sells brooms. The people in the market recognized the police!"

Her voice was thick with rage now, her Spanish so heavily accented by her native Mayan tongue that she was hard to understand. She shook her right index finger at the general. Mejía Victores puffed and puffed. Next to him sat a colonel, smug and disinterested, in sunglasses the color of the polarized windows of the death-squad vans.

"Virgilio was not involved in anything, not the guerrillas, not politics. He was a seller of brooms!" said the Indian woman. "In the name of God and the Santisima Virgin, I ask you, Mr. Chief of State, to free Virgilio!"

Mejía Victores remained impassive. When the last GAM member had spoken, he stood, his mighty paunch pressing against a black leather holster. "You are in the house of Guatemala," he began sanctimoniously.

"Every Guatemalan has the right to petition, and we are disposed to listen." He said he lamented the state of violence that had gripped his country for 20 years—as if the problem were malaria or river blindness. "Let us work together to resolve the problem in the best manner."

The women applauded heartily because their entreaties had reached the chief of state and they had been admitted into the Hall of Mirrors. The general stood to leave, and the toadies of the press hurried over to pump his hand and seek some hoped-for personal recognition. Then he exited through a paneled door, and the three-hour meeting was over. The women of GAM filed out, and the charged air that surrounds a person of great power returned to normal.

The meeting with the chief of state, and everything else GAM did, never resulted in the release of a single disappeared relative. But the group's fearless, pioneering advocacy work had the effect of emboldening other human rights organizations to step forward and demand accountability.

By 1984, Ginny and I were tired of the killing and tired of living in fear. Our phone was tapped. We were occasionally followed. We'd had it. The final straw was when I contracted typhoid after a foolish swim in a coastal river. Every foreigner who lives in Latin America comes down with something infectious sooner or later, what Marlow calls in *Heart of Darkness* "the playful pawstrokes of the wilderness."

Within a week, I was lying in a bed in the Hospital Centro Medico, bleeding through a hemorrhaged duodenum and shedding weight. The days became a haze of enemas, endoscopies, blood transfusions, and stocky Mayan nurses popping their heads in to inquire, *"Como esta el popó*, Señor Juan?"

Ginny was my Florence Nightingale. She kept my spirits up, talked to my doctor, called my parents, prayed with me, and slept in a green easy chair beside my hospital bed every night.

The antibiotics finally kicked in. Four nights after my discharge from the hospital, I brought Ginny out onto the balcony of the apartment where we then lived. Down on the street, a mariachi I'd hired for the occasion struck up our favorite cumbia, *El Africano*. Still in my Centro Medico pajamas, I fell down on one knee and popped the question. She said yes. We held each other tightly and savored our private concert, as did the delighted security guard across the street.

After I was strong enough to travel, we left Guatemala and moved to Atlanta, where she accepted a teaching position at Emory University and I began freelancing for NPR.

In the years after we left Guatemala, I came to believe that some of my acquaintances had fallen under a sort of malediction. Peter Wolfe was the first to die. Then, in 1988, Barry Sadler accidentally shot himself with his own pistol while riding in the back of a cab with a woman in Guatemala City; he died the next year. And in 1991, my old traveling companion, Anson Ng, by then a stringer for the *Financial Times*, was found shot to death in the bathroom of his Guatemalan apartment; the crime has never been solved.

Guatemala continued to pull at us. Over the years, I looked for a complete telling of the story I knew was there but hadn't been able to unearth as a journalist. The whole truth finally came out after a United Nations–negotiated peace agreement officially ended Guatemala's internal armed conflict in 1996. Human rights activists sought a tabulation and a reckoning of the violence that had killed an estimated 200,000 people over 36 years. They conducted meticulous detective work—searching newspaper records, culling archives of victims' organizations, and taking direct testimony from survivors. Forensic anthropologists traveled into the highlands to conduct exhumations and study skeletons for causes of death.

The story of Guatemala's dirty war is contained in three separate reports compiled by a coalition of civil society groups—the International Center for Human Rights Research, the Catholic Church's Recuperation of Historical Memory project, and the UN's Commission on Historical Clarification. The UN report, the most comprehensive of the three, does not exonerate the guerrillas. It concludes they kidnapped hostages for ransom; they murdered military informers, farm administrators, and deserters; and, worst of all, they abandoned sympathetic peasants to the brutal retribution of the army. But the commission attributes 93 percent of the violence to the Guatemalan state and asserts that its response was "totally disproportionate" to the military force of the insurgency. The authors conclude: "None of us could have imagined the full horror and magnitude of what actually happened." Neither could I.

The Big Lie has been exposed. Guatemalans fully realize what their government did during the counterinsurgency war. In the years since the peace accord, insurgents have come forward to join political parties, and the army has returned to its barracks, though it's now openly vilified by many of the citizens it swore to protect.

On a trip back to Guatemala in 2004, I traveled to the upland town of Rabinal, the place where in the early 1980s soldiers and paramilitary allies massacred hundreds of Achi Maya—even children— they suspected of helping the guerrillas. I had come to report a story about reconciliation after the long civil war, and I was curious how Guatemalans were coming to terms with the atrocities. I found my answer inside the recently vacated army base on the outskirts of town. Someone had scrawled in black letters, *"Aqui, estuvieron los demonios."* Here, were the demons.

SECTION II

HACKS AND FIXERS

Chapter 5

KOSOVO:
FIELDS OF NIGHTMARES

WHEN A BIG STORY breaks overseas, there commences a convergence of foreign correspondents to that hot spot that I call *the descent*. It happens with remarkable similarity on any continent. A hotel is unofficially designated as the media beehive. In Sarajevo, it was the Holiday Inn; in Baghdad, the Al Rashid Hotel; in San Salvador, the Hotel Camino Real. In June 1999 in Pristina, Kosovo, it was the Grand Hotel, one of the great misnomers of the international hospitality industry. A correspondent for the *Observer of London* once wrote that the Grand's five stars stood for spooks, thugs, hookers, hacks, and cockroaches.

The foreign press descended on Kosovo to cover the aftermath of the last European war of the 20th century. Earlier that winter, Serb soldiers and paramilitaries had attempted to "ethnically cleanse" Kosovo Province of all ethnic Albanians. A coalition of NATO countries led by the United States, fearing another Bosnian nightmare, bombed Serb positions for three months before Yugoslav president Slobodan Milosevic withdrew his army from Kosovo. As Serb soldiers and Serb families fled in long convoys toward Belgrade, reporters poured across the borders of Macedonia and Albania and through the smeared glass doors of the Grand.

For years, the 10-story, state-owned monstrosity had been a

symbol of Serb domination. Serbian armed forces ran their foreign press center on the second floor. The lobby was a hangout for paramilitary skinheads who considered foreign journalists scum. The notorious Serb war criminal, Arkan, had been a regular guest. A sign on the door reportedly read, "No dogs, No Albanians."

By the time I arrived, the tide had turned. The beleaguered Serb hotel staff, aware they belonged to the losing side of the war, glowered at us all from behind the front desk. The darkened lobby stank of tobacco smoke, stale sweat, and a foul stream emanating from a clogged toilet. Harried journalists stood in clusters on the grimy carpet, breaking into huzzahs on recognizing a familiar face.

Stiff from a five-hour convoy and desperate for a bathroom, I approached a friendly-looking Reuters photographer and asked him where I might find a functioning loo. He pointed in the direction of the Macedonian capital from which I had just come and growled, "Skopje."

Wartime had not improved the Grand's amenities. It had no electricity or running water, and it was badly overbooked. Fortunately, NPR European correspondent Sylvia Poggioli, who reported from Pristina during the Serb withdrawal, had left her room for me. I dropped my gear there and headed back down the hallway. A Spanish newspaper reporter was fiddling with his room key, standing next to an aromatic pile of rotting garbage. I stopped and we chatted, and I asked him whether conditions in the hotel were better in peacetime. "It has always been a shit hole," he roared.

Since I had never worked in Kosovo before, the first order of business was to find a fixer and translator. People don't realize how much of what they learn about foreign news involves this invisible but indispensable link in news gathering. In unfamiliar countries where a journalist doesn't speak the language or know the system, a fixer is gold.

He or she can be a local journalist, university student, teacher, or doctor—just about anybody who speaks good English and is savvy. Because the pay is good and a war economy offers few opportunities, these folks are usually happy to drop what they're doing to work with a foreign correspondent for a few months. They set up interviews, arrange housing, find drivers, locate the safest routes, talk us through military checkpoints, and find the right officials to bribe. Good fixers are jealously guarded and passed along to other reporters the way inside traders share stock tips with friends.

Fixers are often the people to whom journalists on foreign assignments grow closest. They shape what we learn about that country. We end up interviewing their friends and government contacts, we eat with their families, and in the long hours we spend together we learn their life stories and they, ours. We get into and out of scrapes together. They sometimes risk their lives for us.

I walked back into the grim lobby of the Grand where a dozen prospective fixers sat smoking at greasy, glass-topped coffee tables. The first one I approached was a Serb in a black jacket with a pale, fleshy face who gave his name as Dushko. "Would you like a guide? A hundred dollars a day," he said in barely understandable English. He told me he was a student who knew the city, but he struck me as too old for the university, plus he was creepy. I passed.

Then I saw a short-haired, worried-looking young woman in a leather coat that was too large for her thin frame. She was extinguishing one cigarette while she lit another. I introduced myself. Her name was Xheva Berisha. She told me she was an out-of-work Albanian journalist who had waited out the last few terrifying weeks in her apartment with her husband, a hospital internist, and their two small children. Her English was decent, and her eyes had a brightness that appealed to me.

Many reporters had to hire two interpreters. Given the ethnic hostilities, Serbs would often refuse to talk to an Albanian translator, and Albanians were usually too intimidated to talk openly to a Serb. My fellow NPR reporter in Kosovo, Andy Bowers, contracted a Serb university student named Daniela and an Albanian journalist named Jeton. "Each morning, I had to decide which one would get the most honest answers from the people I planned to interview, like choosing the right golf club for a difficult shot," Bowers said.

Xheva's biggest selling point was that she was bilingual. She spoke such fluent Serbo-Croatian that she could often disguise her Albanian blood. I hired her at $100 a day, plus $50 for her friend Tony to drive us. "You won't be sorry," she said, her face suddenly excited by the prospect of some income. "I know my country very well."

I admired the armored yellow Land Rover the BBC tore around town in, but Tony's rattletrap Lada would do. With Xheva in the backseat and Tony at the wheel, we ventured into rural Kosovo to see the results of the Serbs' ethnic cleansing. It was a beautiful, sun-washed early summer, but the recent Serb atrocities kept recalling the nightmare of the spring. The smell of dead livestock machine-gunned by soldiers wafted across fields splashed with scarlet poppies and wild amaranth. We saw bridges still covered with leafy branches Serbs had used to hide them from NATO bombers.

Flocks of black-and-white jackdaws flew overhead as Albanians sharpened their scythes to finish the wheat harvest that had been interrupted by the exodus. We met a smiling, toothless Albanian farmer walking toward us with a Frisbee-size antipersonnel mine dangling from his hand. He was one of the lucky ones. The unlucky ones bled to death in the golden fields of waving grain.

Unlike other reporters who had reported in Sarajevo and understood the Bosnian Serbs' capacity for savagery, this was my first exposure. But there was a familiarity to their handiwork. I'd seen the results of a scorched-earth strategy 16 years earlier in the highlands of Guatemala.

In Kosovo, the Serbs had torched and looted mile after mile of Albanian houses and businesses. On the wall of a gutted service station, Serb soldiers left graffiti for the family of the American president—"Clinton Fac Yu Madr, Clinton Fac Yu Celzi." In an Albanian art gallery, they had slashed the paintings, thrown them on the floor, trampled them, and painted crude pornographic scenes on the walls as their calling card.

The Serb booby traps were especially clever. They were set to kill or maim returning Albanians engaged in the most mundane activities: slipping a tape into a VCR, climbing the back steps, cultivating the garden. Mines, which were cleared through the heroic efforts of international aid groups, seemed to be everywhere. Luckily, Tony knew the trick of scanning a dirt road for fresh tire tracks before proceeding.

On one such lane, we stopped at a brick farmhouse with a red-tile roof where a group of people stood in the barnyard. They had been among 3,000 Albanian residents of the town of Zhabel who had fled to the mountains for more than a month. They fashioned shelters of branches, ate boiled corn, and dug trenches to protect themselves from Serb shelling. A Kosovo Liberation Army (KLA) field hospital treated shrapnel wounds.

The group had just come down from the mountains to the farmhouse to see what had become of its occupants, an elderly couple who were too old to run to the hills. A thin, sunburned man in a filthy sweater directed Xheva and me to a pile of manure in the barnyard. From it protruded a shriveled human hand. It looked unreal, like a movie prop. Serbs had murdered the old couple and buried them in compost.

Xheva tried to translate but was overcome with emotion. "They say they are sad for the loss of their neighbors," she said, sobbing, attempting to regain her composure, "but they are happy that there are no more Serb police in town."

An older man with a deeply lined face and red-rimmed eyes stepped forward. "That is the hand of my brother in that cow shit," he said. "How can we not want revenge?"

The ethnic cleansing of Kosovo was the last act of the Serbs under their fiercely nationalistic president, Milosevic, who was later tried for war crimes and died before he could be convicted and sentenced. In 1989, following the decline of the Soviet Union in Eastern Europe, he sought to unite all ethnic Serbs in the adjoining republics of the former Yugoslavia into "Greater Serbia." As a means to achieve their patriotic ideal, the Serbs launched various military interventions to drive out non-Serbs and bring them under control of the Serbian capital of Belgrade.

Serbian-Kosovar hatred is an interethnic conflict—like Israelis and Palestinians, Tutsis and Hutus, Turks and Armenians—that Americans understand intellectually but don't grasp how deep it runs. Serbs ruled the southern province of Kosovo until the 14th century and thereafter considered it the cradle of their identity. It was there they fought their self-defining battle in 1389 on the plain of Kosovo Polje against the Ottoman Turks, and it was there they erected their most revered Orthodox churches and monasteries.

But Albanians also claim this blood-soaked land. They insist their ancestors, the ancient Illyrians and Dardanians, were here before the Slavs. They point to the fact that the Muslim Ottomans ruled Kosovo for 500 years until 1912, when the Serbs retook it. By that time, the population was predominantly Muslim Albanian, and the stage was set for a long and violent struggle between the opposing nations.

The American psychoanalyst Vamik Volkan defines ethnic hatred as the condition when a people's "we-ness" turns deadly, and they kill for the sake of protecting and maintaining their large-group identity. That is what happened in Kosovo. Serbs nurtured an almost genetic hatred toward the majority Albanians and, moreover, feared that large Albanian families would overpopulate and ultimately destroy the Serb presence.

In 1999, Milosevic decided to use the same tactics against ethnic Albanians in Kosovo that his military employed against the break-away republic of Bosnia-Herzegovina: mass execution, rape, the burning and looting of homes, the destruction of crops and livestock, hunger, and exhaustion. NATO claims that Serb regular and paramilitary fighters executed at least 5,000 Kosovars during this period. The United Nations High Commission on Refugees estimates ethnic cleansing drove 90 percent of Kosovars from their homes. The largest number fled across the border to their ethnic homeland in the blighted nation of Albania, which is where I picked up the story.

During the NATO bombardment of the Serbs, it was nearly impossible to report from inside Kosovo, so hundreds of foreign journalists clustered in the remote border city of Kukes, Albania. The big story was the tens of thousands of Kosovar refugees streaming across the Albanian border to escape the rampaging Serb military and NATO bombings. NATO later reported its bombs inadvertently killed 1,500 civilians.

Albanian families rode in wide-eyed silence in wagons pulled by farm tractors and piled high with household belongings. Once across the bridge in Albania, they flopped onto the ground like exhausted marathoners. Humanitarian aid workers brought them water, apples, and high-protein biscuits.

The refugees told stories of incomprehensible cruelty. There was the Serb platoon that kept a house full of Albanian women as sex slaves in the Kosovo town of Dragocina. The women were forced to strip naked and serve the soldiers food. Every night a soldier entered their room with a flashlight, selected a young woman, and brought her to the garrison to be gang-raped. Afterward, the men tipped her with chocolate. "We have seen terrible things, and we have lived these terrible things," an old woman named Sherife Trole told me from her tent in a mud-choked refugee camp.

Kukes was a backwater in European communism's most forlorn and isolated country. Recently emerged from a half century of dictatorship under Enver Hoxha, Albania was ill prepared for the refugee crisis. Mafiosi and bandits ran amok. A series of national pyramid schemes had bilked millions of Albanians of their life savings. The national symbol was the hundreds of thousands of concrete pillbox bunkers that dotted the countryside, evidence of Hoxha's paranoia that his neighbors would invade at any moment.

Kukes was so small that there were no hotels. NPR had rented an apartment in a shabby brick tenement from an unemployed, thickly whiskered Albanian named Alberto. He was so eager for income that when he heard our offer, he simply took his wife and child out of the flat and handed over the keys.

Humanitarian relief groups estimated that 60 percent of the refugees driven out of Kosovo were children. They were everywhere, playing soccer with empty plastic bottles, hitching rides on the backs of wagons, and sucking strawberry jam out of food aid packets. Every day, kids played on a rusted Ferris wheel in the center of Kukes. The game was to see who could climb to the highest cross brace, then dangle happily with both hands as the wheel began to turn. As the father of three children, I couldn't decide which was more unsettling—the refugees' tales of woe or the playground tragedy waiting to happen.

Many of the children had lost homes or seen family members murdered, and their journeys out of Kosovo had been arduous. I was deeply impressed by the work of the United Nations Children's Fund (UNICEF) in Kukes. Teams of trauma counselors organized games in which the kids expressed what was bottled up inside them. The counselors gave them paper and markers and told them to draw whatever they wanted.

A dirt-smudged Albanian girl drew a series of pictures portraying her family's eviction from their village. There were soldiers, houses aflame, wagonloads of people on the move, and bodies lying on the ground.

"Where is this person's head?" a social worker asked gently.

"The Serb soldiers cut it off," the girl responded matter-of-factly.

A lovely 13-year-old girl with matted blonde hair said her father had joined the KLA, the guerrilla force fighting for Kosovo's independence. "Somebody told us he has been killed. We don't know anything about him. I haven't seen him since a week before we left Kosovo," she said, sobbing.

The UNICEF counselor put her arm around the girl. "You must all remember that when somebody's father or brother is far away, just as you think of them, they are thinking of you," she said.

In sharp contrast to the pathos of the refugees, the hacks never lacked for high spirits. We gathered day and night at a café called Restaurant Amerika that served cold Tirana beer and a passable pasta with marinara sauce. A caged parakeet beside the door somehow survived clouds of smoke emitted by throngs of European journalists. KLA rebels in smart black uniforms who came in to check out the female correspondents set off a terrible commotion among journalists competing to buy them rounds of beer. Everyone wanted to buddy up to the guerrillas to get the scoop on where the fighting was. The rebels drank our beer and enjoyed their momentary rock-star popularity.

The story in Kukes evaporated as soon as Serb forces pulled out of Kosovo. Journalists streamed across the border to personally investigate the crimes. We couldn't get out of Kukes fast enough, and in short order that once forgotten border outpost was again forgotten.

Day by day, the Grand Hotel became incrementally more habitable.

After the power was restored, the elevators sometimes worked. "One day I was on deadline for *All Things Considered*. I pushed UP and it went down. I had the feeling I was on a voyage to nowhere," recalled my colleague Melissa Block.

Food appeared in the restaurant in the form of massive gray slabs of potato salad and what appeared to be slices of fat marbled with hints of meat. (We cheered when Albanians began reopening their restaurants, serving up delicious Ottoman-inspired pastries filled with meat and cheese.) The dining room conversation also made the food hard to digest. Journalists traded stories of what they'd seen—what one called "a promiscuity of violence."

"There were five Albanian kids in the house, and the MUP [Serb secret police] sat them down on a couch with their mother and hosed them all. The couch was drenched in blood. A UN guy thinks it may qualify as a crime against humanity," said a British newspaper reporter at the next table.

In peacetime, reporters spend a lot of time looking for gripping stories to tell. In wartime, the story is so big and unfolds so fast that it sweeps over and around us, like a river of news. In Pristina, all we had to do, literally, was step outside our rooms.

The night of June 27, 1999, the KLA liberated the lobby bar of the Grand Hotel. A group of self-styled guerrillas from New York City calling themselves the Atlantic Brigade swaggered into the dimly lit lobby.

Black-shirted rebels poured shots of Johnny Walker Red for the jubilant reporters and aid workers who bellied up to the bar. It would be our version of the night in 1944 when Ernest Hemingway famously liberated the bar of the Hotel Ritz in Paris.

But the liberation of the bar at the Grand would have a practical purpose. When the Serbs were in charge, they had fired all the ethnic Albanians from their jobs at hospitals, mines, universities, and the Grand Hotel. "We're here to make sure the Albanians who used to work here get their jobs back," a member of the Atlantic Brigade said with a thick New York accent.

As word spread of the KLA party, Albanians drifted in to dance to folk music inside the once forbidden lodge. The festivities didn't last long, though. At 10:00 p.m., British peacekeeping troops announced last call and informed the cheering Albanians that the hotel's Serb director had agreed to meet with former Albanian employees to discuss rehiring them. Once the Grand was no longer off-limits, Albanians came and went as they pleased while the Serb staff skulked about.

The stories that Xheva and I were discovering invariably involved Serb aggression and Albanian victimization. Xheva seemed energized by our work because she detested Serbs. Her husband, a doctor, had been fired from a Serb-run hospital, and she had experienced countless acts of discrimination. I yearned to find an example, just one, that defied this polarization. I wanted a story of two people whose relationship transcended ethnic hatred. That story came to me from Xheva herself. One afternoon, over tea in her apartment, she told me about Kosovka.

Kosovka was a Serb kindergarten teacher and single mother of two small children. She lived two floors below Xheva in the dreary, Communist-era tenement in which we were sitting. Over the years, Xheva and Kosovka struck up a friendship notwithstanding the suffocating class status that marked most Serb/Albanian relations. They found there was more that united them than divided them. Over coffee and L&M cigarettes, they talked of motherhood and agreed never to discuss politics.

During the 77 days of NATO bombing raids, Xheva and her family were the only Albanians who chose to remain in the apartment house. When the explosions shook the walls, she covered her children's ears, stroked them, sang to them, and tried not to show her own terror. As the weeks passed, her friendship with Kosovka became a lifeline. Kosovka let Xheva use her phone to call her sister in Sweden and assure her that she and the family were okay. Kosovka warned Xheva the day Serb police planned to come door-to-door looking for Albanian men, so Xheva's husband would have time to hide. On days the streets were too tense for Xheva to go out and buy groceries, Kosovka brought her bread.

After the bombing, everything changed. Albanians grew confident and belligerent; Serbs became frightened and uncertain. Xheva cried the day Kosovka left for the bus station to take her two children to Belgrade. "She told me she'd be back in a month, and if not, then I should come visit her one day in Belgrade," Xheva said.

Before she left, Kosovka gave Xheva the key to her flat and asked her to watch it for her until Kosovka returned. One day soon afterward, a KLA soldier showed up in the stairwell in front of Kosovka's door. A nosy neighbor had told him Xheva had the key. He demanded she hand it over. "She will be back," Xheva answered. "She has worked all these years to have this flat. I am not speaking good for her because she's a Serb; I'm speaking good of her because she is a good person."

The KLA guerrilla said, "The Serbs burned my house. They killed my father and my son. Are you cooperating with the Serbs?"

Xheva continued, "If I give you a two-year-old Serb child, will you murder him?"

"Certainly not. That's what the Serbs did to us," he replied.

"Then why do you do these things? It is the same," Xheva said.

Despite her pleas, the soldier kicked in Kosovka's door and moved in. In fact, he was there as we spoke. Xheva pointed her eyes in the direction of the downstairs apartment and shrugged her shoulders. "I believe Serbs and Albanians can live together, but it will take a long time," she said. "People have seen so many bad things. They're not thinking with a cool head."

The Albanians had their revenge. The story evolved in the months and years after I left. In an effort to drive out every last Serb and establish an independent Kosovo, Albanians, particularly the KLA, employed some of the same brutal tactics used against them. News stories described Albanians perpetuating the cycle of ethnic hatred, of executions, grenade attacks, arson, and expulsions, sometimes against elderly and unarmed Serbs, and gypsies who had allied themselves with Serbs. Human Rights Watch denounced Albanian marauders, just as it did Serbs in years past. The few remaining Serb villages, which make up less than 10 percent of Kosovo's population of two million, survive tenuously under the protection of KFOR peacekeeping troops.

After I returned home from the Balkans, I wondered if Xheva ever visited Kosovka in Belgrade, if they're still friends, and if the Albanians are running the Grand Hotel any better than the Serbs did.

Chapter 6

PAKISTAN:
BEASTS AND HELLIONS

A S WE WALKED BRISKLY toward the demonstration, my fixer, Hasan, called over his shoulder, "Stay close. If anyone asks where you're from, tell them you're Canadian."

Young Muslim men chanted, "Crush, crush, USA!" and inclined their torsos with each syllable for emphasis. Hasan and I waded into the throng, smiling politely. We found a spot at the edge of the crowd of 6,000 protesters, directly over a trickling open sewer and in front of a dental clinic advertised by a ghastly smiling mouth.

I've stuck out in crowds all my life, but nothing compares to being the tallest American at a Death to America rally.

Street demos were a standing Friday afternoon assignment for journalists bivouacked in the border city of Peshawar, Pakistan, during the fall of 2001 after the attacks of September 11. At the conclusion of afternoon prayers, students streamed out of mosques and into the streets to hear fiery speakers damn the Pakistani and American presidents.

It was my first Friday in Peshawar, a teeming border city of smugglers, refugees, and exiled warlords located at the historic Khyber Pass on the Afghan border. The city, whose ethnic Pashtuns deeply empathized with their kinsmen across the border, was aflame with anti-American sentiment. US warplanes were pounding the Taliban in Afghanistan, and Pakistani newspapers ran daily pictures of bombed civilian houses and bleeding Afghan children. The images had electrified Muslims who swore to join the Taliban and help defend Islam. A few Pakistanis actually did. Untrained and ill equipped, they were slaughtered by battle-hardened Tajiks of the US-backed Northern Alliance. But mostly the *jihadi* wannabes stayed in Pakistan, where they fulminated at rallies like this one, then went home and studied their physics textbooks.

"WE WELCOME TERRORISM IN ALL ITS FORMS," read a placard in blood-red Arabic. The scene couldn't have been more different from my assignment a month earlier at ground zero in New York City. At the Jacob Javits Convention Center, I interviewed a rescue captain from the Baltimore Fire Department who, blinking back tears, told me of finding a group of dead NYC firefighters, their arms linked around each other as the second tower collapsed on top of them. New Yorkers uttered the name Osama bin Laden as though it were a strain of hemorrhagic fever. Here on the other side of the globe, his face was plastered on T-shirts under the slogan "Osama, the Great Mujahid [holy warrior] of Islam."

Far at the front of the assemblage, a speaker was bellowing into a cheap microphone that distorted his voice so much, it reminded me of the punk rock bands I used to hear in Austin. "He is saying America is the worst terrorist in the world," Hasan said as I scribbled in my notebook, "and that Afghanistan will be their graveyard."

I noticed then that a pudgy, flush-faced student had hoisted a homemade sign directly over my head that read "Americans Are Uncivilized Beasts and Shameless Hellions." It was printed in English, no doubt for the benefit of CNN.

"Hasan, tell this man to take his sign down," I said.

"Just ignore it, John."

"It makes me nervous."

"No one will hurt you. It's okay."

I stared at the student and he stared back at me, expressionless.

"Then tell him I really like his sign and I'd like to have it," I continued.

"What?" Hasan glanced at me.

"Ask him if he will give it to me as a gift."

I'll never completely understand why the student complied. Perhaps he wanted to show me he was neither beast nor hellion like my countrymen, or maybe he thought I needed to meditate further on his message. For whatever reason, he rolled up the posterboard and handed it to me with a smile.

And then he said, "You are our brother, no problem." He extended his hand to shake mine. "You are our friend, no problem."

"I am your brother?" I asked.

"Yes, you are our brother," he repeated.

Dumbstruck, I wanted to visit further and find out why he was so friendly, but a crowd had gathered around us—never a good idea at an emotional rally. Hasan said it was time to leave. I followed his bobbing head through the swarm and back through the narrow streets of the Khyber Bazaar, where boys hawked plugs of sugarcane and cups of green tea.

"Hasan, what just happened back there?" I asked.

"Muslims hate US foreign policy," he explained patiently, "but people of the Northwest Frontier Province are very courteous to foreigners. We are Pashtuns. Our tradition is hospitality."

After that unexpected encounter, I spent the rest of my six-week assignment in Pakistan trying to understand the Pashtuns and their tribal honor code of Pashtunwali. My guide through Pashtun culture was Hasan Khan, a 28-year-old Pakistani journalist who held a master's degree in English literature from Peshawar University. His favorite author was Emily Brontë. He was so blond and blue-eyed that he would have been mistaken for a westerner were it not for his *salwar kameez*, the loose-fitting tunic and trousers favored by Pakistani men.

Hasan was the perfect fixer. He seemed to know someone everywhere we went, from plainclothes policemen to real estate agents to industry officials to expert sandal makers. His gentle, self-deprecating humor was a welcome antidote to the constant zealotry around us. On a warm, late-November afternoon, at another emotional rally in the frontier town of Mardan, Hasan translated the speaker: "Satan depends on technology; God depends on the faith of Muslims . . . Death to USA . . . Long live Islam. Those who are friends to America are traitors." Without missing a beat, he shot me a grin and added, "I am one of them, John."

In Peshawar, the beehive was the Pearl-Continental Hotel. The lobby was decorated like a Raj-era palace, with the syrupy sixties hit "Love Is Blue" playing on a tape loop. Pakistani spooks and wishful fixers hung out in overstuffed chairs.

On any international story, the hacks try to situate themselves as close to the action as possible, but not so close that they can't get cocktails after deadline. The PC, as the Pearl was known, had the only semipublic bar in the city—the sign next to the door stated, "Non-Muslims & Foreigners Only." My first visit convinced me the tavern was meant as a punishment for infidels who desired a fermented beverage. It had all the charm of a shipping container. The only beer available was a watery brew called Murree's, made at a 140-year-old brewery originally established for thirsty British troops when Pakistan was part of the empire. I asked the bartender who his clientele was today, and he replied contemptuously, "Christians and Sikhs."

The Peshawar press corps tended to separate into peer groups, which I suppose is human nature. It happens on every story. The Japanese keep to themselves and possess a knowledge of the story that is inversely related to the number of pockets on their khaki photojournalist vests. The European journos hang out together drinking coffee, smoking cigarettes, and never seeming to have deadlines. American and British correspondents, bound by a common language, tend to socialize together.

The starkest divisions between journalists are not over nationality but medium: There's TV, and there's everybody else. One veteran hack I know defines a story's critical mass as the point "when TV comes." In Peshawar, Japanese TV crews paid $300 for a room that had been $85 the previous week.

The advent of 24-hour news networks has created a new breed of television reporter—the "dish bunny." Attractive, dashing, and mellifluous on camera, in practice, he or she rarely leaves the sweeping vista of the rooftop live shot. Instead, the dish bunny allows field producers to gather footage and take the tenor of the streets. Once I was eating with colleagues in the hotel restaurant when a correspondent for an American network whose name rhymes with "pox" pulled up a seat and unloaded, "I've been on the fucking roof for a week, so what's going on in this country?"

News gathering is sausage making—not for the squeamish. In the PC lobby one afternoon, I overheard a breathless British television cameraman, a red kaffiyeh rakishly wrapped around his neck, who'd just returned from an Afghan refugee camp. "The last shot is fucking incredible," he said to his colleague. "He's got flies in his mouth and his eyes. He looks dead, but he's alive. Incredible, man."

Journalists try to convey reality but invariably we distort it, none more so than photographers and videographers. In the Pearl bar one night, I mentioned this observation to a friendly Irish TV cameraman as we sipped Murree's.

"I know what you mean," he said. "I spent five years in Northern

Ireland. We'd wait two hours through a peaceful demonstration for one car to be burned. TV loves a burning car. But it gives the impression that burning cars are all over Ulster, and they weren't."

I described my experience at the anti-American rally, about how the protestor had given me his sign and warmly shaken my hand. I filed an audio postcard on the experience for *All Things Considered*, and the response I received was overwhelming. Our listeners appreciated having their stereotypes of crazed militants exploded. According to TV images, all of Pakistan was a powder keg, which it wasn't. A Peshawar matron told me she and her neighbors were so frightened by the pictures on Pakistani evening news that they were afraid to go to the bazaar.

"So what do you want, pictures of picnickers in the park? You just don't get it, mate. This is TV," said the Irishman.

In some ways I envied the photographers. Peshawar was such a visual story, especially the kaleidoscopic streets. Pelotons of bicyclists sped past with their *salwar kameezes* fluttering behind them. Wagoners, standing upright like charioteers, drove donkey carts laden with cordwood. Hand-pedaled tricycles bearing disabled Afghan war veterans weaved in and out of traffic. Elaborately painted freight trucks, like rolling works of folk art, rumbled past. On the shoulder of the boulevard, camel caravans plodded along, aware only of the switch of the herder. At intersections, street kids came by with tin cans of burning herbs. For five rupees they swung homemade censers inside of cars, leaving pungent smoke to ward off evil. Puttering about everywhere were the three-wheeled, motorized taxis called rickshaws. Their tailgates usually bore one of two images: the grimacing, muscled Pashtun action hero, Badar Muneer, or a pair of seductive, kohled eyes—Pakistan's version of the chrome babe silhouette mud flaps.

"Why the eyes?" I asked Hasan.

"That's all we see of a woman, and so that's what attracts us," he said in another of his patient tutorials. "For me, Muslim women create suspense. Western women show everything to a man. There's no suspense."

Ever since arriving in western Pakistan, I had been curious about the role, or lack of it, of women in Pashtun society. Everyone had seen pictures from Taliban-controlled Afghanistan in which women were forced to wear the head-to-toe, sacklike garments called burkas. But I was surprised to see virtually every woman in the streets of Peshawar wearing a burka. Journalists took to calling them BMOs—blue moving objects. The only women's eyes I saw on the street were on the backs of rickshaws.

When I asked Hasan why women voluntarily wore burkas, he told me airily that no one forced women to don the garments; they chose to wear them out of modesty and to protect family honor. But if the burka was supposed to douse male sexual attraction, it seemed to have the opposite effect. Hasan and our driver Mushtaq, a meek Pashtun who became predatory behind the wheel, picked me up one windy morning and announced that this was their favorite kind of day. Why would they say that, I asked, with all the dust and fecal material flying through the air?

"Because the wind shows a woman's form under the burka," Mushtaq replied gleefully.

Pashtun men considered the reputation and chastity of Pashtun women to be inviolable. They reserved their lust for western women, or, lacking that, Punjabi women from eastern Pakistan. The video stores did a brisk business in DVDs featuring chunky Punjabi women in thick black eye makeup, waggling their enormous bottoms at the camera.

Journalists covering the guerrilla war against the Taliban made the same observation of the Muslim Tajiks of the Northern Alliance. To reach the battle front, reporters had to travel for three days over the rugged Hindu Kush mountains to a remote mud-brick village where the Northern Alliance had set up its field camp. In order to ease the privations, a savvy engineer for an American TV network showed Northern Alliance officers how to position their satellite dish to download Russian porn from the Hotbird satellite network. From then on, the engineer always had a seat on a chopper to visit outlying war camps.

Tired of the stifling Pearl pub, I set out one night to find the American Club, which supposedly had a proper bar and would admit credentialed US correspondents. I flagged down a rickshaw and climbed into the back, and we lurched into traffic. The driver, a hooknosed Afghan in a traditional white cap and vest, began to sing. Ten minutes later, he was still singing. Twenty minutes later, he continued spinning off verses, one after another, mournful, beautiful, and numberless. I started my tape recorder.

When we arrived at the American Club, an officious Pakistani guard at the entrance told me I couldn't come in because I didn't have embassy security clearance. At that moment, a corpulent, pink-skinned man in a polo shirt walked into the bar, stopping briefly to look me up and down. Suddenly, I realized I would much rather listen to the singing taxi driver than join a table full of American consular officers. I ran out to catch the musical cabbie before he left. On the way back to the PC, I recorded another 20 minutes of his soulful singing.

The next day I played the tape for Hasan and asked him what the words meant. He told me it was a *tappa*, an improvisational Afghan folk song sung in Pashto, the language of the Pashtuns. "All Pashtuns are poets," Hasan said, enjoying the tape as much as I was. "The driver is singing to an imaginary girl: 'I am from Kandahar, and I love you. Let us go out together hand in hand. If our love succeeds, then we will live together forever. But if we die, we will be together in death forever.'"

and was relatively open about it. He'd been baptized here and was a member of our evangelical team. His own family shot him as an honor killing. He left a wife and four children." He looked down at the Oriental rug on his floor and then back up at me. "We feel quite insecure at the moment. But what can we do? We cannot step back from the mission given to us."

In a matter of weeks, the Taliban fell, and the press corps abandoned Peshawar and the Pearl-Continental and raced across the border to Afghanistan. But the bombs drove out only the Taliban. The ancient code of Pashtunwali, impenetrable like the stone canyons where Pashtun tribesmen dwell, remains as strong as ever.

ABOVE: Grand Hotel, located in downtown Pristina, Kosovo, June 1999 (Courtesy John Burnett)

BELOW LEFT: Bus art, streets of Peshawar, Pakistan, October 2001 (Courtesy John Burnett)

BELOW RIGHT: Columned house in flooded Plaquemines Parish, Louisiana, September 2005 (Courtesy John Burnett)

ABOVE: Qudrat Andar and Shafi Noorzai, NPR fixer and cook, on tank with unidentified Northern Alliance soldier, Kabul, Afghanistan, February 2002 (Courtesy John Burnett)

LEFT: Carlos Garcia, the leaf player of the zocalo, Mexico City, June 2001 (Courtesy John Burnett)

ABOVE: Two unidentified soldiers (with machine guns) belonging to the militia of warlord Padsha Khan Zadran, Paktia Province, Afghanistan, February 2002 (Courtesy John Burnett)

BELOW LEFT: Zalmai Yawar (standing alone in black jacket and cap), fixer and translator, Kabul, February 2002 (Courtesy John Burnett)

BELOW RIGHT: Katrina evacuee on Crescent City Connection Bridge, August 2005 (Courtesy John Burnett)

ABOVE: Iraqi youths slapping donkey with "Saddam" written on its hide, Sadr City, Baghdad, May 2003 (Courtesy John Burnett)

BELOW: Mushtaq, driver (left), and Hasan Khan, fixer (right), in front of restaurant, Peshawar, Pakistan, October 2001 (Courtesy John Burnett)

ABOVE: Three Iraqi men in public school, Baghdad, Iraq, May 2003 (Courtesy John Burnett)

BELOW: Marines on the road to Baghdad, southern Iraq, April 2003 (Courtesy John Burnett)

ABOVE: Author with Gun Crew 3, Eleventh Marine Artillery Regiment, First Marine Division, in the southern Iraq desert, April 2003 (photographer unknown)

TOP RIGHT: (Left to right) NPR correspondents Eric Weiner, Michael Sullivan, and John Burnett with "Uncivilised Beasts" sign, Islamabad, Pakistan, October 2001 (photographer unknown)

TOP LEFT: Don José Elías Sánchez (in plaid shirt), Granja Loma Linda, September 1992 (Courtesy Katie Smith Milway)

TOP RIGHT: Carroll Pickett spent 15 years as the Texas death house chaplain, counseling 95 men who were put to death (more than any other prison chaplain in America). (Courtesy Pat Stowers)

BELOW: Manolo Martinez, January 1993 (Courtesy Will Van Overbeek)

ABOVE: Novice bullfighter at la tienta on Martinez's Rancho Guadalupe, January 1993 (Courtesy Will Van Overbeek)

BELOW: Toros bravos, fighting bulls, running in the fields, January 1993 (Courtesy Will Van Overbeek)

Chapter 7

AFGHANISTAN: MEN WITH GUNS

OUTSIDE THE DARKENED TERMINAL of Kabul International Aiport, a young man with a prematurely aged face and wearing an NPR cap extended his hand. "Hello, Mr. John, welcome to Afghanistan," he said.

Qudrat Andar, our 28-year-old fixer, led me to a battered Dodge Dart and tossed my luggage in the trunk. I climbed in the front seat, and the driver threaded his way through crowds of bearded men in woolen cloaks. Then he pulled onto the boulevard leading into the shattered capital. I had never seen a city, a people, or a land so exhausted by war. Every building and every face revealed the agony of the last 23 years, during which a million and a half Afghans died in conflict after conflict.

I was finally here. It was February 2002. Four months earlier, I had been watching from across the border in Peshawar, Pakistan, waiting for the Taliban to fall. Now I was anxious to see what was left of Kabul. In the southern precincts of Kabul, we drove past neighborhoods reduced to rubble, everything broken or mangled or splintered, with an occasional family peering from a windowless structure. In the distance, the majestic, snow-covered Hindu Kush range glowed as white as a wedding dress, but the city that stretched out before us was despoiled.

"You cannot imagine what we have lived through," said Qudrat, finally, from the backseat.

Kabul Province was an archaeological site of war. The devastated neighborhoods I was looking at had been pulverized a decade earlier during the mujahedin war. Before that, the Soviets destroyed roadside villages south of the city. Then the Taliban wiped out grape vineyards on the Shomali Plain north of Kabul. Then US smart bombs obliterated Taliban military installations. A forensic entomologist might compare Kabul to a corpse feasted on by successive arrivals of insects.

I felt grateful to be visiting the capital during this pause in its violent modern history. After the US Air Force and a ground force consisting of Tajik and Uzbek fighters belonging to the Northern Alliance had driven the Taliban out in November 2001, Afghans seemed to be venturing outside after the end of a long storm. Hundreds of thousands of refugees were returning from Pakistan. With the Taliban gone, television repair shops and video movie outlets quickly opened. Kites fluttered above houses again. Tea shops and kebab stands were crowded.

People walked the streets with growing confidence, celebrating but not entirely trusting the newborn peace. The evildoers were still around. Afghanistan's "Kalashnikov culture," the tendency to settle differences with assault rifles, was still intact. To be reminded of the continued danger, one had only to look in the menacing faces of the gunmen who lounged every day outside the guesthouse of Abdulrab Rasoul Saif, a fundamentalist *mujahid* who had once vowed to raze every house in Kabul that didn't face Mecca. I saw them every day because Saif's henchmen were our neighbors.

During the first months of postwar Kabul, NPR and the Voice of

America (VOA) shared a house in the upscale Wazir Akbar Khan neighborhood. The two-story structure was as cold as a cave, but it had electricity and occasional hot water. My housemate was Gary Thomas, the veteran VOA correspondent who arrived in Kabul like a Victorian dowager just off a transatlantic steamship. From steel cases and black duffel bags he pulled cheese, wine, single malt Scotch, a portable stereo, and a collection of Doc Watson and Norman Blake CDs. Thomas was excellent company. We both learned as much about Afghanistan from the amazing house staff as we ever gained from interviews.

Qudrat was a medical student who claimed to have been the national chess champion before the Taliban outlawed chess. He had a ruggedly handsome face, always wore a black leather trench coat, and guarded his emotions like a good chess player. His strategic thinking was a useful quality in a fixer. When we needed to bribe someone to get electricity at the house, Qudrat knew the city employee at the junction box to pay off. When I needed a four-wheel-drive vehicle to take us to the mountains, Qudrat showed up with a car and driver.

My predecessor in Kabul, Peter Breslow, senior producer of *Weekend Edition Saturday*, had given the whole house staff NPR caps. They wore them with great pride. Upon entering a government office, Qudrat would announce to the startled bureaucrats, "We are *NPR!*" It helped that we had come, not from Australia or France, but from the country whose B-52s had hammered the Taliban in retribution for 9/11. Afghans respect might and revenge. One morning at a militia checkpoint when two Northern Alliance soldiers spent a few minutes too long inspecting our passports, Qudrat suddenly yelled, "Let us pass, you donkeys! We are riding with the owners of this country!" Queasily, we drove on.

Our other translator was a 26-year-old engineering student named

Zalmai Yawar. Zalmai was tall and lanky, with thick eyebrows and a prominent nose. His English had a wonderful lilt and energy. To my ear, Zalmai put his stylistic touch on every radio interview he translated. He had a playfulness that was lacking in many young Afghans who had lived through so much bloodshed and privation. One time we all stopped to have our picture taken by a "MINES" warning sign beside the highway. When I developed the photo, there was Zalmai feigning a dive into the minefield. His whimsy was all the more remarkable when we heard what had happened to him during the civil war.

In 1992, five mujahedin warlords began a ruthless and greedy war among themselves for control of the capital. The title mujahedin, or Islamic holy warrior, was a holdover from their leadership in the CIA-backed guerrilla war against the Soviet occupation. By the early nineties, most Afghans considered the mujahedin anything but holy. Their idea of warfare was to randomly shell the opposing sector of the city from surrounding hillsides in the hope of killing enemy soldiers or civilians. It was a time of indiscriminate death. Men who walked to the market for naan, a round piece of unleavened bread, were struck down by flying shrapnel that seemed to come out of nowhere. Thousands died this way, out of the blue, as if by Rapture.

Zalmai's family is Pashtun, the same majority ethnic group to which a brutal warlord, Gulbuddin Hekmatyar, belonged. But the Yawar home was located in a Pashtun neighborhood in a section of the city controlled by the Persian-speaking Hazaras, who were fighting Hekmatyar. Hazaras are descendants of the Asiatic Mongols who swept through Afghanistan with Genghis Khan in 1219. Like many Pashtun families, the Yawars fled to the provinces to escape fighting in the capital. As the eldest son, Zalmai, then 17, was appointed to stay and house-sit to prevent anyone from looting their belongings.

Conditions steadily worsened. One day a Pashtun man who lived across the street was led away by armed Hazaras. They returned later the same day carrying a sack containing the two halves of his body severed at the abdomen. Zalmai watched from his window as the man's wife stood over the blood-drenched sack, wailing and beating herself hysterically. But he and other neighbors were afraid to help her bury her husband, fearing they would be next. "After that day, whenever there would be a knock at the door I thought my turn had come," Zalmai wrote in an unpublished memoir.

Every time Zalmai went to the market for milk and naan, he risked forced conscription by Hazara fighters. Once he was taken off a bus at gunpoint and brought to the Hazara front line, where he was forced to stack sandbags while enemy bullets hit the ground around him. Another time, he was accused of spying and taken to a Hazara prison. The jail was located next to a brick kiln that was said to be used to burn prisoners who belonged to rival militias. When his captors could find no evidence against him, they took him to the southern front, where he was compelled to strip building materials from vacant houses. A friendly Hazara commander eventually negotiated his release and sent him home.

"In that time, you simply did not have any control over your life. Boys as young as 12 years old had guns, and they would stop you and ask you anything. You could not disobey them without risking your life," Zalmai wrote.

Zalmai spent more and more time inside his parents' home. To relieve the boredom, he began to collect books from a plentiful and unexpected source. Hazara gunmen could be found on the roadsides, selling burlap sacks full of books they had looted from the Kabul University library. In the struggle for survival in war-torn Kabul, books had become raw material. Pages were torn out and pasted together to make sacks. Shoemakers cut up the bindings for soles. The going rate was 700 afghanis—about 16 cents—for 15 pounds of books, whether it was *Weight Loss Made Easy* or *The Complete Works of William Shakespeare.* "In those times, books were more valuable as household goods than as literature," he wrote. "It was very sad to see so many good books destroyed."

Zalmai rescued books by the kilo, hauling them back to his house, where he discovered the joys of English literature by the light of a kerosene lamp. He read *The Ugly American, Shiloh, The Rise and Fall of the Third Reich, 1984, The Quiet American, Darkness at Noon,* and his favorite, *Travels with Charley.*

"I would collect the best ones and put them on the scale and buy them with some of the money that was sent to me for food. I made a new cover for the books at home. Because I was alone, I kept myself busy reading. The books gave me heart," he told me later.

The fighting in his neighborhood intensified. During a pitched battle in February 1993, a mortar round landed inside his house, and shrapnel ripped through the wall behind which he was hiding. He woke up at the hospital with a piece of shrapnel in his thigh and burns on his face. When Zalmai left the clinic, he went directly to Logar Province to join his worried family, who was overjoyed he was alive. But Zalmai felt despair. "By this time our house, which was unguarded for several weeks, had been looted. We had lost literally everything—all our furniture, books, clothing, and family photographs," he wrote. "All those troubles I had gone through for nine months had been for nothing."

But he was wrong. His love of learning and sacks of books served him well. Everybody at NPR who worked with Zalmai fell for him. After his tour of Afghanistan, Scott Simon helped Zalmai get into Amherst College in Massachusetts, where he is, at this writing, working on a geology degree.

After the brutality of the mujahedin war, Afghans initially cheered the armed force of young Koranic students who emerged in 1994 calling themselves the Taliban. Though the Taliban had a harsh reputation for Islamic Puritanism, at least they were restoring order and driving out the hated warlords. But Kabulis soon realized they had traded one demon for another.

Under an extreme version of Sharia law unheard of in the Muslim world, nearly all entertainment was outlawed, and joy itself was suspect. The new rulers banned television, theater, music, movies, card games, kite flying, and any depiction of the human form in art, advertising, or child's play. Dolls were snatched away and snowmen kicked in, with the warning, "These are idols."

The despised, black-turbaned agents of the Ministry for the Prevention of Vice and Promotion of Virtue policed the citizens of Kabul for the slightest infraction. Men were forced to attend the mosque five times a day, grow beards, and, in a bizarre interpretation of the Koran, shave their pubic hair.

The Taliban applied their cruelest fiats on women. Girls' schools were closed, and women were fired from all places of employment. After all female dentists and doctors were dismissed, women had no one to treat a toothache or gynecological problem because they were forbidden to see male doctors. Women were not allowed to go out in public without a male relative as an escort, so half a million women who had lost a husband or an elder male relative in the decades of war became prisoners in their homes.

"No force could stop us when we saw the hunger and thirst of our children," said Gulalai Habib, a Kabul schoolteacher I interviewed in Peshawar. "We would come out, and the Taliban would beat us with leather lashes. But we would go and beg, go to the UN and beg for food. We could not stand to watch our children cry."

When women ventured outdoors, they were required at all times to wear the burka. Femininity itself was effectively outlawed. "If a woman came out with an ironed burka or a white head scarf, the police would ask us why we ironed it. 'Just wear a rough burka. Don't show yourself,' they told us. 'Why is that scarf shiny?' These were all laws they made," said Habib, a big-boned woman whose eyes possessed a quiet ferocity.

Inside a clandestine school on a back alley of Peshawar, Habib introduced to me one of her students, a sweet-faced 14-year-old, named Besira, in an olive head scarf. When she began telling her story, her eyes became wild and expressive. "On hot days we would sweat under the burka. It was so hot, it took your breath away. We could not see our footsteps, and sometimes we would trip over the burka and fall and hurt ourselves. Nobody was allowed to raise the burka to eat ice cream. That was before they closed the ice-cream shop because they served girls," she said.

Zaina, a soft-spoken 22-year-old Hazara from Bamiyan in a white head scarf and shapeless black dress, was listening, and she chimed in: "We were alive, but our soul was taken from us. When I went to bed, I prayed to God to destroy the Taliban; I prayed to God to let them burn in hell."

Everyone in Kabul had amazing stories about life under the Taliban, including our staff at the NPR/VOA house. Our cook, Shafi Noorzai, was a husky 19-year-old with a goofy smile and a sweet temperament who was recently engaged. He was trying to earn $2,000 to pay the steep expenses of an Afghan marriage, which included a wedding party, a marital bed, jewelry for his fiancée, and carpets for her family. He was grateful that his cousin Qudrat had gotten him the job because he didn't know how to cook. Shafi was a competitive kickboxer.

"Shafi," I asked him one day in the kitchen, as he was cooking a chicken in the pressure cooker, "what's that nasty scar over your eye?"

As he told it, the Taliban defense minister had heard about his expertise in kickboxing and asked him to teach the fighting art to his bodyguards. During sparring one day, a bodyguard got carried away and Shafi responded in kind, injuring the aggressive student. The defense minister was furious. He authorized his henchmen to beat young Shafi with their rifle butts. He felt fortunate to escape with his life.

Of all the stories I heard about the Taliban, those that Qudrat told had the quality of perverse Bible stories.

The Parable of the Laughing Fornicator

There was a man who had sexual relations with a woman not his wife. The Taliban punished him by pouring black dye on his head and parading him through the streets of Kabul in the back of a pickup. Along the way he began to laugh. A furious Taliban policeman demanded, "Why are you laughing?" The man answered, "Because I saw my father, and he could not recognize me."

The Parable of the Bicycle Thieves

Once the Taliban arrested a man who stole a bicycle. They took him into the stadium to cut off his hand, the standard punishment for thieves. In those days, many people came out to watch the Taliban carry out criminal sentences because there was little else to do. After the spectacle concluded, the spectators left the stadium and realized that thieves had stolen all their bicycles.

The Parable of the Unfortunate Talib

Once a Talib was beating a woman on the sidewalk for revealing her ankles below her burka. Instead of begging for mercy, she became enraged and screamed at him, "Your father is a donkey, and your mother is a dog!" The defiant woman fled. The Talib gave chase. The driver of a speeding truck saw the black-clad agent pursuing the woman and swerved to run over him. When the policeman investigating the death questioned- the truck driver, he said, "I never saw any Talib."

After the Taliban melted away, Afghanistan still faced a dilemma—what to do about rival warlords. Afghanistan is not so much a country as a conglomeration of fiefdoms, each ruled by a bearded man in a turban who travels with a retinue of riflemen packed in the bed of a Toyota Hilux pickup. Their job is to look menacing and assist the master in his various tasks, which may include but are not limited to smuggling opium, exacting tribute, and shelling the neighboring chieftain.

In the news of the day, what these tribal titans did was important because their cooperation or truculence determined how the new US-backed Afghan president, Hamid Karzai, governed his disparate nation. Plus, warlords make great copy if you can land an interview. One of the more colorful and accessible chieftains was Padsha Khan Zadran, who had an unparalleled reputation for corruption and brutality within his realm, the remote and rugged border provinces of Paktia, Paktika, and Khost.

Khan was a cunning and ruthless player of Afghan realpolitik. After the Taliban fell, Karzai had briefly appointed Khan as governor of Paktia, a deeply traditional province in eastern Afghanistan. But the president changed his mind after local officials rejected the imposition of the unpopular Khan. Meanwhile, US commanders had enlisted Khan as a strategic ally because his border territory was interlaced with hidden trails said to be used by Taliban and al Qaeda fighters. The CIA had reportedly given the illiterate warlord a satellite phone and underwritten his ragtag army with a briefcase full of greenbacks.

Khan's first stunt was on December 20, 2001, when he used his influence with the Americans to call in a US air strike against a column of rival tribal elders who were traveling to Kabul for Karzai's inauguration. Khan claimed the travelers were al Qaeda and Taliban fugitives. American rockets killed dozens of elders and villagers, which infuriated locals and embarrassed the US military.

Khan struck again on April 27, 2002, when his militia indiscriminately rocketed the provincial capital of Gardez. He was still sore that authorities there were preventing him from taking what he believed to be his rightful seat as governor of Paktia. Scores died, mostly innocent civilians. President Karzai took to calling Padsha Khan a murderer.

As a reporter, I wanted to meet the infamous godfather of Paktia and ask Khan what his next move would be. My traveling companion was Cox News Service's Lou Salome, a nonpareil newspaperman who celebrated his 61st birthday in Afghanistan. While most correspondents working in South Asia favored the rugged outdoor look of REI, Lou wore the journalist's regulation trench coat, corduroys, and Dockers, despite being 12½ time zones from his newsroom at the *Palm Beach Post*. I packed my shortwave radio and a large jar of crunchy peanut butter and stuffed a sack full of national currency—at the time, a 10,000-afghani bill equaled 35 cents.

With Qudrat's help, I hired a taciturn Pashtun driver named Haji

Sefiullah who wore a diamond-patterned sweater over his *salwar kameez* and sported a beretlike woolen cap called a *pakool*. His rattling Toyota Land Cruiser was as much of a survivor as he was. In the waning days of the Taliban, Sefi had simultaneously outrun a pursuing Taliban commander and evaded machine-gun fire from a US warplane that mistook the speeding Toyota for an enemy vehicle. Having lived to tell the tale, he thought nothing of chauffeuring two Americans into a remote border region filled with Taliban sympathizers in search of Padsha Khan. "If God wills it, we shall find him," said Sefi, with a mischievous smile.

It was a relief to flee bombed-out Kabul and finally take in the countryside. Rural Afghanistan is a starkly beautiful place, reminiscent of the craggy stone peaks, luminous sky, and unending vistas of the Big Bend country of West Texas that my friend Marion Winik once described as "taking a hike through the mind of God." We passed old men stooping under great bundles of bound herbs, a teenage boy hunting ducks with an 1858 British flintlock rifle, and villages that consisted of nothing more than mud-walled tea stands and Russian shipping containers enjoying a second life as tire-repair shops.

Well-off Afghans lived in adobe compounds surrounded by tall walls and guard towers that gave them the appearance of frontier forts—for good reason. This was tribal country, Pashtunwali country, a land of men with guns, a place where tribesmen shouldered Kalashnikov assault rifles "the way other men wear wristwatches," a Pakistani doctor told me. And they didn't just carry firearms; they decorated them like fashion accessories. They rolled metallic green and red tape around the magazine clips and buttstocks of their rifles. They hung plastic beads from the barrels and attached colorful stickers on the steel surfaces. In Khost, I met a guard who had a plastic rose attached to the sight of his rifle—like a national guardsman at Kent State. Afghan gun art was everywhere.

Every time we crossed a frigid mountain pass, we entered the dominion of a new warlord. Checkpoints were manned by hard-faced men in woolen cloaks and *pakools* who stamped their open-toed sandals in the snow. They conducted desultory searches of the Toyota, usually demanded a bribe, and, if they were in a good mood, invited us into the guardhouse to warm ourselves by the stove and drink tea.

On the road to Gardez, we met several former soldiers of Padsha Khan who gave us our first refreshing glimpse of Afghans repudiating the Kalashnikov culture. Six men took us into a small room heated by a brazier and poured tea, seemingly happy to abandon their guard post to chat with foreigners.

"What's it like being in Padsha Khan's army?" I asked.

"I am tired of fighting and keeping guns. We want a national army. I have carried a gun for 23 years. We are thirsty for peace. I want to open up a shop in the bazaar. I'll do anything," said a man named Semargol, who rested his assault rifle across his lap. I recognized in his eyes—deep set, wary, and weary—the same look I'd seen in Qudrat and countless other Afghans. The violent history of modern Afghanistan was etched in their faces.

As we drove through the lunarlike landscape, I kept spotting great wooden spools suspended over holes in the ground. This was the equipment of the *kariscans*, the tunnel diggers. In order to bring water to the village from a mountain watershed 10 miles distant, villagers had long ago tunneled by hand to the water source, like human moles. Access wells were dug every 90 feet or so. Every spring when the snow began to melt, townsmen carried oil lamps and shovels and lowered themselves down the wells to clear the miles of *karis*.

"Five years ago, four people were killed in our *karis*. Last year, one person died. My grandfather was killed in this well," said a tall, weather-beaten man named Haji Gulam Hussain whose bushy beard was dyed red with henna in honor of the prophet Muhammad.

Noiselessly, far above, a US Air Force B-52 Stratofortress traced delicate twin contrails in the ice-blue sky. I thought about all the communication gear, radar equipment, smart bombs, and other 21st-century gadgets the B-52 was carrying. And I looked back at the well digger, whose son was down in the *karis* filling a rubber sack with mud, using technology that was biblical.

"Why don't you ask a nonprofit to get you a pipeline and a pump to bring water from the mountain? It would be much less work and a lot safer," I told the man.

He smiled, revealing a row of stained teeth. "A pump will break, but the *karis* is forever."

Our search for Padsha Khan quickened when we reached the warlord's checkpoint and picked up our first guide, a man named Rahmatullah. He said he would take us to Khan's guesthouse. When he told us he was a general in Khan's army, Lou asked him if he'd ever killed anybody. "I fired a rocket once, and I don't know what happened. It landed far away," he said sheepishly.

We traversed snow-covered high desert that reminded me of northern New Mexico, even down to the construction of the adobe homes. When we got to Khan's guesthouse, he was gone. An old man in a tattered sweater and vest climbed in the car and said he would lead us to Khan's home, where we might find him. Sefi expertly maneuvered the Toyota through tracks in the bumper-deep mud. When we finally arrived at the next house, which looked a lot like the guesthouse we'd just left, Khan wasn't there either.

This time, a boy of about 10, his cheeks flushed from the early spring chill, told us Khan was meeting with tribal elders in Sayyed Kalam, "not far from here." I exchanged glances with Qudrat, and he shrugged. The boy squeezed into the Toyota and sat on the first guide's lap, and we all bounced along a dry riverbed toward the next destination.

In rural Afghanistan, all decisions of consequence are made in unfurnished rooms ringed with cushions on which men sit cross-legged, drinking copious amounts of green tea and expectorating into tin spittoons. It was in such a place that we finally found Padsha Khan, Central Casting's version of a warlord. A scowling man in his mid-fifties rose to greet us. "*Salaam aleikum* [peace be with you]." "*Aleikum salaam* [and peace be to you]," we responded. But he did not look like a man of peace. His eyes were the color of the bullet casings that lined the bandolier across his chest, and his bushy mustache was as black as the turban wrapped around his enormous head.

The 40 men sitting in the circle were a *shura*, or council of elders, that represented 11 tribes of Paktia Province. They were all turbaned, well armed, and prolifically bearded. We greeted each of them individually.

When he spoke, Khan deftly tuned his comments to his presumed audience, his American benefactors, from whom he clearly wanted more money. "I am 100 percent behind the American action in Afghanistan," he said grandiloquently. "I am fighting against al Qaeda. If the UN and the US do not help us, it would be treacherous against us."

"But why should the United States support a warlord with a reputation for brutality?" I asked him. I felt 40 pairs of eyes on me. Padsha Khan's face darkened.

"I have worked for six years to bring peace and security to my country," he said, his voice rising so that all the elders could hear. "It is not good to call me a warlord. It is the word my enemies call me."

After a 15-minute interview, Padsha concluded with the statement that under his benevolent but firm hand, his territory was safe and free of al Qaeda. He offered to send us with his driver to inspect his stronghold, but we declined. I was already beginning to feel a condition familiar to journalists, a quickening of the heartbeat, a tightening of the chest, that I call deadline arrhythmia. It signals that no matter where you are on the planet, no matter how much or how little material you've collected, regardless of whether you've eaten or slept, there is an editor at his or her desk—in this case, 7,900 miles away at 635 Massachusetts Avenue—waiting for you to file. As an old hand at NPR once said, "It's time to feed the maw."

At the end of my six-week assignment, I needed to buy a present for my wife, whose generous willingness to stay at home with our three children allowed me to take this far-flung trip. But what was there to buy the woman in your life in post-Taliban Kabul? In Afghanistan, nothing says "I love you" quite like a brand-new burka, so Qudrat and I headed to the bazaar.

The burka seller, an oily man with bad teeth and eyebrow dandruff, beamed when he saw me—another American journalist looking for a souvenir. Sensing a big sale, he flew around his stall pulling out burkas in colors once forbidden by the Taliban: canary yellow, chartreuse, and magenta. I noticed three women watching me from the street. They were each wearing a threadbare burka in traditional cornflower blue. What were they thinking behind those veils?

Suddenly I felt guilty. How could I buy these garments of oppression as a joke? Were the women cursing me? Or were they covetous of the gaily colored garments laid out before me? None of the above. As soon as I finished my purchase and stepped into the street, they stuck out their hands and pleaded piteously for spare change. I handed each a wad of afghanis and hurried out of the bazaar.

As I was leaving the marketplace, eager to get back to start packing for my long flight home the next day, I spotted a man in a tattered police jacket holding a sharp steel rod in one hand. Curious, I asked Qudrat to ask him what he was doing. The man cheerfully explained that he was a parking attendant. When he found a car parked too close to the bazaar, he jabbed the shank into the tire as instant punishment for the owner. He proudly pointed to a taxi cab with a flat rear tire.

"If the idea is to keep the area clear of cars," I said to Qudrat, "why is he disabling vehicles? It doesn't make any sense."

"Mr. John," Qudrat said, smiling, "you are finally beginning to understand Afghanistan."

SECTION III

ROGUES AND HEROES

Chapter 8

THE DEATH HOUSE
CHAPLAIN

ON HIS FINAL DAY, Stephen Ray Nethery read for an hour and a half; refused recreation; ordered a last meal of two cheeseburgers, french fries, and milk; and requested a last visit with his father, mother, sister, uncle, and a minister. Nethery had been on a Texas death row for 13 years. The 33-year-old Tennessean was being put to death by the state of Texas for his crime on a February night in 1981. A young Dallas policeman, John McCarthy, had surprised Nethery while he was having sex with a girl in his car parked by White Rock Lake. Nethery was drunk and high when he climbed out of his vehicle buck naked, leaned over the hood, and reportedly said, "Officer, I'm sorry," before firing three shots at the cop.

At 11:52 p.m. on May 26, 1994, I was among the six media witnesses who gathered in the wood-paneled waiting room outside the busy Texas death house in Huntsville. An atmosphere of tense routine prevailed. "Y'all get much rain out there?" asked a big-bellied guard in a gray uniform, trying to keep the mood upbeat. "Not much," answered the prison public information director, a tense man in a gray sport coat who was nearing retirement. A roaring air conditioner in the window held off the steamy East Texas night. A thin, fine-featured reporter from Swedish TV whispered to me, "I'm scared."

At 12:19 a.m., the guard's phone rang.

"They're ready," he said.

We passed through three chain-link gates and a heavy gray door, then filed into a small room dominated by a window into the blue-walled death chamber. There was Nethery, strapped spread-eagle to the T-shaped gurney with IV tubes running into both arms. Pallid and handsome, the inmate stared at the ceiling and licked his lips. The scene, bathed in cold fluorescent light, was so startlingly ritualistic that I half-expected an Aztec priest to step up and cut out his heart with an obsidian knife.

The warden, looking grave in a blue blazer, called for the final statement.

"Well, I just want to ask people to pray for the two grieving families," Nethery began in his Tennessee drawl, "my own family and the family of Officer McCarthy. I appreciate the prayers for both of 'em. Praise God for his grace and mercy. Thank you for letting me come to Jesus. Lord Jesus, receive my spirit. Amen."

With that, the warden removed his glasses, the signal for the lethal chemicals to flow. Two executioners behind a one-way mirror each plunged a series of syringes.

Nethery shut his eyes and swallowed hard. His masticatory muscles quivered. He exhaled. His lips turned pale blue. All movement ceased. Someone in the death chamber coughed. There was complete silence in the witness room.

The doctor, an emergency room physician with a well-trimmed beard and cowboy boots, leaned over and shined a penlight in the cop killer's eyes. He put a finger on his carotid artery, then a stethoscope to his unbeating heart. Inmate number 698 was pronounced dead at 12:30 a.m. He'd simply gone to sleep, never to awake. Lying on the gurney, Nethery's last images of this world would have been a black microphone suspended from the ceiling with the word "Realistic" on the side and the kindly face of Rev. Carroll Pickett, the death house chaplain.

That night in Huntsville, I couldn't get to sleep. In my hotel room—a state-owned facility built of red bricks by inmate labor—I talked on the phone with Ginny about the unsettling experience of watching a healthy person be put to death. I found myself thinking about Pickett's role in the execution the same way I did the death house doctor; both men had taken oaths to uphold a greater good, to nurture life at all costs, but were somehow complicit in this grim business of death by government. What I didn't understand was that, at the time, Pickett was engaged in a profound struggle within himself over the rightness or wrongness of what he was doing. But he didn't dare disclose his doubts. He waited until his retirement the following year.

After counseling 95 doomed men—more than any other prison chaplain in America—Pickett eventually became an outspoken opponent of the death penalty. Coming from deeply conservative roots in a small South Texas town, his was a remarkable journey.

When Carroll Pickett was growing up in Victoria, Texas, in the 1940s, no one questioned capital punishment. His father, R. C. Pickett, the Victoria County superintendent of schools, taught his six children that severe infractions deserved severe punishment. Execution was the law of the land. It had been for as long as anyone could remember.

Early on, Pickett had wanted to continue the family vocation and become a schoolteacher. He thought about teaching algebra and coaching tennis. But in 1950, after starting a youth choir at his church, he grew interested in Christian education. Four years later, after college, he enrolled in a Presbyterian seminary with the simple desire to find a small country church where he could preach, baptize, marry, and bury. One of his seminary professors told him presciently, "You're going to be around death a lot."

Though the Presbyterian Church formally opposed the death penalty, Pickett remained a staunch supporter of capital punishment, his conviction strengthened by a tragedy in his own First Presbyterian Church of Huntsville. On July 24, 1974, an infamous San Antonio drug lord named Fred Gomez Carrasco and two accomplices began the most notorious prison siege in Texas history. They took 10 prison employees hostage inside the prison library and announced their intent to escape from The Walls, the old, fortresslike, red-brick penitentiary in downtown Huntsville. Two of their hostages were women who attended Pickett's church. "They sat two rows apart in my congregation, and I knew them well," he said.

On the 11th day of the standoff, the inmates and their hostages made a break for a getaway car in a homemade Trojan horse fashioned from two blackboards lined with law books to absorb bullets. The prison riot squad attacked the group with fire hoses, hoping to disorient them enough to free the hostages. But in the ensuing gun battle, the inmates executed both women hostages and wounded a third, a Catholic priest. The task fell to Pickett to deliver the news to the families that the two women were dead. "After that, if I ever wavered, I was pretty strong in favor of the death penalty," he said.

In 1980, Pickett was offered a job with the Texas Department of Corrections as chaplain of The Walls. He accepted, thinking he would spend his time meeting the spiritual needs of the 2,200 convicts: preaching, directing the inmate choir, doing bedside vigils at the prison hospital, and burying inmates. Two years later, the warden announced to his stunned staff that Texas was ready to conduct its first execution since the US Supreme Court reinstated the death penalty after a 10-year moratorium. Texas would be the first state to use the new method of lethal injection, believed to be more humane and professional than electrocution, hanging, the firing squad, or the gas chamber. As chaplain at The Walls, home of the Texas death house, Pickett was required to comfort the condemned inmates and their families. Pickett would be the new "death chaplain." He hadn't asked for this assignment, but he accepted it and vowed to do the work as compassionately as possible.

Americans are, by and large, comfortable with the death penalty. It's the ultimate punishment in 38 states, the federal justice system, and the US military. Despite national polls in which a majority of respondents say capital punishment is not a deterrent, that it is applied unfairly across jurisdictions, that innocent people are sometimes put to death, and that life without parole is a more favorable alternative, Americans still choose execution as a just punishment for premeditated murder. We believe that it prevents the killer from killing again and that it is fundamentally fair—an eye for an eye. While support for the death penalty hovers around 65 percent nationally, it's even stronger in Texas, at around 75 percent. Since the death penalty was reestablished in 1976, more than a third of the nation's executions have been carried out in Huntsville.

Like the Kennedy assassination, the death penalty is one of those features of Texas life and lore that looms large to the rest of the world but that we Texans rarely talked about. It was never spoken of in my home in Dallas between my parents, both of whom are native Texans. And yet it was always there. When I was a kid, Old Sparky, the oak chair in Huntsville that delivered 2,000 volts to its unlucky occupant, was a state symbol—like Davy Crockett's flintlock rifle or a Texas Ranger's revolver—that embodied our toughness. We take care of troublemakers. If you kill a cop in Texas, you'll go down, too. Capital punishment has never lowered the crime rate one whit, but Texans seem to find great reassurance in its existence.

For a Texas-based journalist, the death penalty is a story that periodically rears its head, every time a celebrity inmate or a controversial conviction goes to the gurney. By the summer of 1994, the quickening pace of capital punishment in Texas had turned the state into a kind of execution assembly line in the eyes of critics. I pitched a series of stories to *All Things Considered* that would try to explain the politics, cost, application, and culture of the death penalty in my native state. How was it that on execution nights, students from Sam Houston State University stood outside The Walls and sang "Happy Trails to You," and a downtown café sold Killer Burgers?

During my research for the series, Rev. Emmett Solomon, former chief of chaplains of the prison system, told me that during the 18-year period when Texas had no executions, juries in certain murder trials were so outraged, they gave defendants sentences of 1,000 years and more. "That ceased when the death penalty came back," he said. "I sense it satiates a great craving on our part to seek poetic justice."

The most unforgettable interview was 82-year-old Sam Gilstrap, the prison's former master mechanic who threw the switch on Old Sparky 125 times. He took a dim view of lethal injection. "He killed somebody else, so why make it easier on him?" Gilstrap said, sitting in a La-Z-Boy in his pink-carpeted living room in Huntsville. "Let him hear that motor kick on. Shake him up a little bit. Let him fight it out."

I had hoped the most revealing interview would be Rev. Pickett, who was popular with the inmates and said to be reflective on the death penalty. But as we sat at a table inside the prison church, Chapel of Hope, he demurred. "In order to do this ministry," he said evenly, "I don't take a position."

Well, at least not publicly. Pickett had already decided the death penalty was barbaric and ineffective, but he couldn't tell anybody because he didn't want to get fired. Today, I think his story matters to me more than anyone else in the death penalty abolition movement. As he wrote in his moving memoir, *Within These Walls*, "I am simply a man who saw the system at work not from the distant vantage point of political office or the halls of academia, but close enough to smell fear's sweat and foul breath."

During my second interview with Pickett after he'd retired, we drank iced tea in the living room of his East Texas home, hung with photographs of his son and six daughters from two marriages. At 76, he had the trim figure of an avid tennis player and the soft voice of one accustomed to speaking about delicate issues. His eyes possessed light and flintiness.

Once he became chaplain for the nation's busiest death chamber, Pickett quickly realized that his one-day ministry, as he called it, was important and profound. Without minimizing the horror of the crimes committed by the men he counseled, he saw his role as living out the meaning of Jesus's words in Matthew 25:40: "Inasmuch as ye have done it unto one of the least of these my brethren, ye have done it unto me." In terms of "the least of these," there are few human beings lower on the scale of humanity than death-row convicts.

The warden of The Walls, Jack Pursley, was also a church-going Christian, but he saw Pickett's role in more practical terms. Pickett said, "Pursley told me, 'Your job is to seduce their emotions so they won't fight coming out of the cell or getting up on the gurney. Anything else you want to do is fine.' "

Pickett took to heart Pursley's instructions to do whatever it took to keep the inmate calm, even though it often involved bending the rules. He'd let the convict have a last cigarette or a cigar in a no-smoking prison.

He'd let him prolong his last phone call or visit. One time, Pickett called a radio station and had the warden delay the execution for three minutes so the inmate could hear his last request, Willie Nelson's "Help Me Make It through the Night."

On that last day, the death house chaplain is the only link between the inmate and the outside world. His last visit with his family, his last phone calls, his last letters, the disposition of his personal items, his funeral arrangements—they all have to go through the chaplain. But Pickett's primary function was simply to be there and to listen, what he calls his ministry of presence. "No one," he told me, "should face dying alone."

In an effort "to search desperately for the good in all these men," Pickett made it a habit not to read about their gruesome crimes. But sometimes it was hard. Some convicts confessed to him rapes and murders for which they were never convicted. Some reveled in memories of sadistic deeds. "One of 'em told me how he raped a girl, then threw her on an ant bed and weighed her down with bricks to watch the ants bite her. Sometimes the stories were so graphic the guards got sick," he remembered.

The anxiety in the death holding cell was unbearable. Some inmates did calisthenics. Some paced. Some got so nervous they threw up or had diarrhea. Many couldn't finish their last meal.

In April 1994, Richard Beavers ordered six pieces of french toast with syrup, six barbecued spare ribs (though he never got them; inmates only get what's available in the prison kitchen), six pieces of bacon, four scrambled eggs, five sausage patties, french fries, two pieces of yellow cake with chocolate icing, and four cartons of milk. When the huge repast arrived on three trays, Beavers was too scared about dying to finish it.

Ronald Clark O'Bryan, the infamous "Candy Man," murdered his eight-year-old son with cyanide-laced sweets on Halloween night for $20,000 in insurance money. The night he was put to death in March 1984, he ordered a T-bone steak (likewise unavailable), french fries, corn, sweet peas, salad with french dressing, and Boston cream pie. "He said he was so tough he'd save his dessert until right before midnight to go out of the world on a full stomach," Pickett said. "But then he was too nervous to eat it."

As midnight approached, Pickett made it a habit to make sure his charge knew exactly what to expect. He told him it was eight steps from the holding cell to the death chamber. He said the room would be cold, like an operating room. The tie-down team would strap the inmate onto the padded table with eight thick leather straps. The executioners would insert IVs into both arms, and they would have 12 sizes of needles available. Bigger needles were best because the chemicals flowed faster; if the inmate was a former drug user who'd burned out his veins, they'd have to use smaller needles.

When everything was ready, Pickett told him, the warden would step outside the chamber to bring in the witnesses, and the convict had 45 to 60 seconds alone with the chaplain to tell him whatever he wanted. That was the point that some men, who'd expected a stay of execution up until the last minute, finally got religion. One asked Pickett to teach him the Lord's Prayer at five minutes to midnight.

"Others would say, 'What do I say when I see God?' I'd answer, 'What do you want to say?' One of 'em said, 'I want to see my two children who were killed in a car wreck.' So I told him, 'Then tell that to God.'"

Pickett tried to rehearse the prisoner's last words with him earlier in the day so he wouldn't stammer or forget them when the time came. "Nine times out of 10, the convict would look at me and I'd nod to him, or we'd have a signal like a wink so he could begin his last statement,"

Pickett said. "He was scared. Now he's close to dying. They're all scared, except for the mean ones."

The first solution is a lethal dose of the anesthetic sodium pentathol, followed by five ampoules of pancuronium bromide to paralyze the muscles, and, finally, 10 ampoules of potassium chloride to stop the heart.

Pickett told them when the killing drugs started to flow, the sensation in their arms would change because the chemicals were a little warmer. The chaplain encouraged them to exhale the wind from their lungs to quicken death, and they should quickly fall asleep in nine to 12 seconds.

He did not tell his charges about the executions that went bad.

In March 1985, technicians probed both arms and a leg of Stephen Morin for 40 minutes before finding a suitable vein. In April 1992, it took 47 minutes for Billy Wayne White, another ex-junkie, to help the team find a vein so they could kill him. In May 1989, Stephen McCoy gasped, choked, and arched his back off the gurney. A state official later conceded the drugs "might have been administered in a heavier dose or more rapidly."

Then there was the infamous "blowout" during the execution of Raymond Landry in December 1988. Because he was so muscular and his veins were burned out from drug use, the needle popped out of his arm and lethal chemicals squirted onto the floor.

"We saw it coming. It wasn't flowing because he had these big Popeye biceps. When he flexed, it just popped out. The warden gave me the signal, and I shut the curtain [to the witness room]," Pickett said. The catheter was reinserted while Landry lay there half dead. The doctor finally made the death declaration 40 minutes after the strap-down.

Despite the well-publicized botched executions, Pickett looked back with pride on most nights, when everything went smoothly. As other states began to legalize lethal injection, they sent their prison

games whose moves are shouted between cells, such as chess or Dungeons and Dragons. "Life on death row is sensory deprivation," inmate Lester Bower told me.

As the years passed, Carroll Pickett began to have gnawing doubts that what the judicial system was doing was fundamentally wrong. The facts about the condemned men that seemed so black-and-white from a distance became much more complicated and conflicting when seen from the intimacy of the death cell. Pickett found disturbing moral dilemmas in what was being done in the name of the people of Texas. He enumerated for me seven problems he had with it.

First, there was age. Pickett counseled 10 condemned inmates who had committed their crimes when they were 17. With teenage children of his own, he knew how impulsive and immature a 17-year-old could be. He concluded their minds were not developed enough to understand the consequences of what they had done.

Second, Pickett noticed that the longer he worked on death row, the larger it grew—from 100 inmates when he arrived to more than 300 when he left: "The more we executed, it seemed, the more were coming to prison. The only one it deterred was that one we killed."

Third, he found himself thinking that some of the condemned convicts were "pretty nice guys" who he wished could live. They had clearly made a terrible mistake in their youth, for which they should pay a severe price, such as life in prison. But he began to think that death was unfair in many cases. Pickett remembered Stephen Ray Nethery, the inmate I watched die, as "gentle as a lamb," a born-again Christian who shared his faith with other death-row inmates. It was easy for a jury to look at a wild-eyed young defendant and agree that his future dangerousness was such that he must be put to death. But after spending an

average of 8½ years on the row, the inmates Pickett met were sometimes different people, remorseful and repentant.

Fourth, the men sentenced to death were not always the trigger
pullers. Pickett said he met several convicts who confided to him their
responsibility for a capital murder but who accepted sentences short of
death in return for testifying against an accomplice. Though it's common practice for accomplices to turn state's evidence, Pickett wondered
whether justice was blind when one guilty man died while the other
lived.

Fifth, there were the dumb ones. Johnny Paul Penry, the murder-
rapist with an IQ of 54, came to the death house on the day of his
scheduled execution with coloring books, crayons, comic books, and no
understanding of what was about to happen to him. In 2000, the US
Supreme Court stayed Penry's execution. Then in 2002 and 2005,
respectively, the high court ruled as unconstitutional the execution of
persons who were found to be mentally retarded and who committed
crimes under the age of 18.

Sixth, Pickett remembered a startling private conversation he had
with the highest law enforcement officer in the state. Then attorney
general Jim Mattox was a pro-death-penalty bulldog who once bragged
in a campaign ad during the 1990 Texas democratic primary for governor, "[Opponent] Mark White carried out the death penalty one time. I
carried it out 32 times." Yet Pickett claims Mattox, who came to The
Walls to witness every execution on his watch, once confided to him,
"Isn't it a tragedy that we have to do this?"

In a 2006 interview, Mattox, now a private real estate attorney in
Austin, conceded to me that the tough-talking 1990 TV ad did not reflect
the actual misgivings he had at the time about the death penalty—the
randomness of its application by local district attorneys, the poor quality
of defense attorneys versus the skilled prosecution teams, the jury selec-

tion process that assures pro-death-penalty jurors, and the transformation that many inmates undergo after long years on the row. Mattox told me he still supports the death penalty in some instances, but his own repeated exposure to the death chamber "causes you to feel a certain level of remorse and sympathy for that individual, regardless of that crime, and causes you to say, 'Isn't there another way to resolve this?'"

Finally, as Pickett continued to walk inmates to the death chamber, he says he could not get around the sixth commandment: Thou shalt not kill. The Walker County death certificates filled out for all executions only reinforced his discomfiture. The cause of death given is "homicide by lethal injection."

"How can Texas kill people to show that killin' people is wrong?" he asked.

The watershed case in which many of his misgivings about the process came together was inmate number 33. Carlos DeLuna was a ninth-grade dropout who had killed a convenience store clerk during an armed robbery in Corpus Christi. Pickett met him in the holding cell the day of his scheduled execution, December 7, 1989. Abused by his stepfather, DeLuna had always craved a meaningful relationship with an older man. On his final day, he took to calling Pickett "Daddy."

Though he was 27 years old, DeLuna, like a child, asked Pickett if the needle would hurt and if Pickett would hold his hand. The chaplain said the rules forbade it, but he would hold his ankle. The strap-down team fastened the restraints onto the wide-eyed DeLuna, the warden gave the signal, and the chemicals started to flow.

"Ninety-nine percent of the time, the sodium pentathol went to work in 9 to 12 seconds, but DeLuna didn't go to sleep," Pickett said, shaking his head at the memory. "He raised his head off the gurney and looked at me with these big old brown eyes."

It didn't go the way Pickett had promised him. Pickett could feel the inmate's pulse in his ankle. DeLuna wasn't dying. The seconds ticked by interminably. DeLuna stared at Pickett with fear and confusion. Pickett nodded to him that everything would be all right, but clearly it wasn't.

Finally, 24 seconds into the execution, DeLuna's head sank back onto the padded gurney, and he died with his eyes open. Pickett, feeling powerless and hollow, stayed with the body until the funeral home attendants came to pick it up. "I felt like I had failed him. It blew me apart. To call somebody Chaplain is one thing. To call him Reverend is one thing. I've been called all kinds of things. But Daddy? That's a term that means 'I trust you a hundred percent.' My kids call me Daddy," Pickett said, his voice growing husky and trailing off.

After the DeLuna execution, Pickett grew depressed and had trouble sleeping. He was unable to put this death watch behind him like he could the others. The searching brown eyes continued to haunt him. Pickett sought therapy for himself with a hospital chaplain he knew in Dallas, to whom he poured out his thoughts about his ministry and his role in capital punishment. "I began to ask, 'What am I doing in this ministry? How many more can I do before I quit?'" he said.

On execution days, the staff of the Brazos Presbytery, of which he was a member, held a morning devotional at which they prayed for Pickett. He always felt like their prayers gave him strength on execution days. But with the death of Carlos DeLuna, it was as though the balance had shifted. He admitted to himself for the first time that what the state was doing was wrong. He came to the conclusion that he was a part of something primitive and unchristian, but there was no one beyond his counselor with whom he could share his revelation.

The counselor told him he had every reason to quit to preserve his mental and physical well-being. Other prison chaplains had refused to be involved. At San Quentin State Prison, site of California's gas chamber, several chaplains asked to be reassigned rather than walk inmates to their death. In fact, the warden, Daniel Vasquez, asked for reassignment after two executions and later became an anti-death-penalty activist.

Death-penalty opponents often demonize the warden and guards who attend an execution. They imagine the prison staff relishing the task of exterminating society's most heinous criminals. But Pickett learned the opposite was true. The death decision rests with prosecutors, judges, juries, and pardons boards. The task of carrying it out falls to decent men and women who have one of the hardest, most thankless jobs in the world.

The image that I had from the witness room of a dispassionate, bureaucratic killing masked the emotional impact the process had on those involved. "You got used to it, but you never got comfortable with it. And you certainly never looked forward to it, watching a healthy person die unnaturally," said former warden Jim Willett, who oversaw 89 executions at The Walls from 1998 to 2001.

Many staffers continued to embrace capital punishment, believing they played a vital though unpleasant role in carrying out the ultimate punishment duly chosen by the people of Texas. But others broke. A guard captain named Fred Allen participated in 130 executions as part of the prison tie-down team before he abruptly resigned and became a carpenter. Allen's story was included in the Peabody Award–winning public radio documentary *Witness to an Execution*, produced by David Isay and Stacy Abramson. Allen said:

> I was just working in the shop, and all of a sudden something triggered in me and I started shakin' and I walked back to the house, and my wife asked me what's the matter. I

said I didn't feel good. Uncontrollable tears were comin' out of my eyes. I thought of the execution I did two days ago and everybody else's I was involved with. And what it was, was something triggered within and all of these executions suddenly sprung forward. . . .

My main concern now is these other individuals. I hope this doesn't happen to them, the ones that do the procedure now. I believe, sincerely, somewhere down the line something is gonna trigger 'em. Everybody has a stopping point; everybody has a certain level. That's all there is to it."

Pickett watched as certain guards, supervisors, and executioners quietly asked to be removed from the execution team. After a few years, he started holding Tuesday-night counseling sessions on the fifth floor of the prison hospital for staffers so they could talk about it. He learned that it was hard for many guards to watch the last family visit, the last meal, and the last shower. It was hard for some guards when the inmate thanked them politely after the straps were fastened. It was hard to kill a likable convict, a man who'd chatted amiably with guards, someone who had obviously changed since his hell-raising days.

Pickett handled the tension as best he could. He played tennis. He talked with trusted advisors. He prayed. When he came home after an execution, his clothes wet with perspiration, regardless of how late it was, his wife, Jane, would have a bowl of banana pudding waiting for him—his favorite.

Pickett retired from the prison system in 1995 and hasn't been back to The Walls since. Ten years later, as we sat and talked on his couch, he wondered if his health problems were somehow tied to his death house duties. He has had a triple bypass and three ulcers, and in 2005, an inoperable four-inch clot was discovered in an anterior coronary artery. "My doctor told me, 'You're gonna pay a price for this.' He said, 'You're too emotional. One of these days your body is gonna rebel.' I took the stress of watching people get murdered as long as I could."

Three years after Rev. Carroll Pickett retired, the state prepared to put to death the first woman executed since the Civil War. It would become the most publicized execution in state history. But there was something special about Karla Faye Tucker.

"Hell, I wouldn't have minded having her as a neighbor," said Larry Fitzgerald, the former prison public information director in Huntsville. "I had dreams about her."

The 38-year-old woman's bubbly personality, toothy smile, bright eyes, and strong Christian faith belied her grisly crime. At 25, she murdered two people with a pickax shortly before she and an accomplice planned to steal motorcycle parts from one of the victim's Houston apartment. High on drugs the night of the crime, she told investigators she got an orgasm each time she swung the three-foot tool into her victim. Further, she described a horrific childhood in which she used heroin at 11 and later became a prostitute. Of her mother, Tucker was quoted in a book about her life as saying, "We used to share drugs like lipstick."

But that was the old Karla Faye. The new Karla Faye, 13 years removed from her crime, charmed everybody who met her—guards, wardens, reporters, evangelists, and especially anti-death-penalty activists. Her popularity helped turn her execution night, February 3, 1998, into an internationally broadcast circus.

The street in front of The Walls filled up with hundreds of demonstrators and journalists from around the world. It had been building for weeks. Televangelist Pat Robertson found himself on the same side as Amnesty International spokeswoman Bianca Jagger in asking Governor George W. Bush to spare Tucker's life. A poll in the *Dallas Morning News* revealed that although 75 percent of Texans supported the death penalty, only 45 percent wanted it applied to Tucker. It was a blatant double standard. She was a woman, she was pretty, and she was charismatic. Lots of handsome, young, contrite men had gone to their deaths with nary a protest. But on the night of her execution, Tucker's fate had come to embody the whole fractious debate over capital punishment.

"The only reason we're paying any attention is that she looks like one of the Brady Bunch girls and not like Granny Clampett," a crime victim's advocate told the *Houston Chronicle*.

Out in the streets, church groups sang "Amazing Grace" while local college undergrads chanted, "No mercy! No mercy!" One young woman held a sign with the words, "Forget Injection. Use a Pickax."

The foreign press lapped it up. They delighted in portraying the Lone Star State as a land of Bible-quoting, tobacco-spitting, gun-toting crackers who believed in Old Testament justice, and the execution crowd didn't disappoint.

To complete the tableau, the prison seemed to have assigned all of its fat, bug-eyed, Copenhagen-chewing guards to the perimeter of the press area. A tall, thin reporter in a trench coat strolled across the prison lawn, smoking what I took to be a Gaullois. "What do you think of Huntsville?" I baited him.

He looked at me pitiably, surveyed the crowd, and said in a heavy old-world accent, "Executions are like football for you people, aren't they?"

And who could blame him for thinking so? All day, the prison public information office had been handing out a 65-page press kit that reveled in the state's ultimate punishment. "Texas leads the nation in executions since the death penalty was reinstated in 1976," it trumpeted. "California has the largest death row population but ranks almost last in the number of executions carried out." *Nyaa nyaah* to those spineless white wine sippers on the West Coast. The strangely comprehensive press release read like a *Guinesss Book of Execution Records*, including every last meal request for the preceding 144 convicts, the youngest executed (24) and oldest (59), brothers executed (5 pairs), longest time on death row (24 years), and shortest (8 months). It reported that lethal injection was a bargain—only $71.50 worth of chemicals. Who wouldn't think my state had a morbid fascination with capital punishment?

TV helicopters hovered overhead. Satellite trucks clogged the parking lot. Television reporters adjusted their lights and solemn expressions. I hated this assignment. I felt like a jackal on a corpse, a 19th-century correspondent to a public hanging. When I talked live with Noah Adams on *All Things Considered* shortly before the execution, I was so rattled I barely caught myself two-thirds of the way into a career-ending malapropism—"Karla Taye Fu . . ."

Inside the death chamber, Tucker gave a final statement: "I love all of you very much. I'm going to be face-to-face with Jesus now." She gasped twice, groaned, and died at 6:45 p.m. with her eyes open.

When a prison official walked outside to announce her death to the throng, students began singing, "Na na na na, na na na na, hey, hey-ey, good-bye."

Then the husband of Tucker's female victim rolled his wheelchair to the microphone and said triumphantly, "I want to say to every victim in the world, demand this! This is your right!"

The execution of Karla Faye Tucker did not have the effect desired by the anti-death-penalty movement. It did not become the galvanizing case that forced a meaningful debate of the death penalty in America.

After the crowds left and the street crews cleaned up, the state of Texas went right on with its pace of executions. In the weeks after her funeral, two supervisors on the execution team and the warden overseeing the process quietly asked to be reassigned.

Chapter 9

THE BULL KILLER

THE THREE YOUNG bullfighters were easy to recognize when they swaggered into the Burger King in Monterrey. With long legs and tight butts, they moved with the graceful cockiness of high school running backs. They ordered Whopper Dobles, and then we all piled into their muddy Ram Charger and peeled out of the parking lot. At the wheel was an impetuous 17-year-old named Antonio Guajardo who passed cars wildly on the left or the right, and I thought we were going to die there on a lonely highway in the rugged backcountry of northern Mexico.

He was eager to impress us and did so with an account of his first goring. "The horn went in two centimeters from my anus, but it wasn't deep," he said casually. "If you haven't been gored, you're not a bullfighter."

Beside the highway, a crosswind inflated the plastic sacks stuck to mesquite trees and barbed wire so that they looked like wind socks. We were on our way to meet the most famous living bullfighter in Latin America, Manolo Martínez. Recently retired, he had set himself up on an 11,000-acre ranch in southern Tamaulipas State and stocked it with fighting bulls from the respected San Mateo brand.

One of the bullfighters repeated my question, "Why was he great? His class. His art. Ummm"—he was having a hard time translating something as intuitive and nonverbal as bullfighting into words—"he gets the bull to obey him. It's almost like he tells it, 'Walk by here.'"

From the backseat, a 17-year-old who fought under the name El Gallo completed the thought: "Manolo Martínez is a maestro."

The truck pulled into the ranch at sunset at such a peaceful hour, it was hard to imagine anything out here was being bred for violent death. From the window I saw herds of *vacas bravas*—mother fighting cows—moving calmly and heavily through their pastures. A deepening violet flooded across the vast Mexican sky, backlighting the serrated silhouette of the Sierra Madre Oriental. The garrulous young toreros fell silent as we walked into a Spanish-style ranch house with a high-ceilinged living room dominated by two enormous mounted bull heads.

The killer of bulls walked toward us across a tiled floor. He was short, light of step, stout of waist, well dressed in a khaki shirt from Eddie Bauer, and uncannily bullish. His black hair curled and kinked like the tousled fur on the broad forehead of the beasts whose heads hung on his wall, and his eyes possessed a cold intensity after facing down almost 3,000 bulls during hs long career. The men in his retinue remained silent, as did an attractive young woman with bleached blonde hair.

"Buenas noches. Bienvenidos a Rancho Guadalupe," Martínez said with reserve. We all sat down on overstuffed leather furniture.

I had been fascinated with bullfighting ever since attending a brilliant series of bouts the year before at the Plaza Mexico in Mexico City. I'd bought a ticket for myself and my cabdriver, a dedicated aficionado who insisted we sit in the cheaper *sol*, or sunny, section because "this is where the people know bullfighting." We drank Corona beer out of wax cups, and he schooled me in the nuances of the *fiesta de toros*. The men and the animals were superb. I was spellbound. At the end of the afternoon, the taxi driver turned his dark Indian face to me and said, "They were good today, but you should have seen Manolo."

After my introduction to bullfighting, on a lark I contacted the

Mexican Association of Brave Bull Breeders and requested an interview with Martínez, who had retired from the sword in 1990. To my surprise, he accepted and invited me to his ranch. I was not disposed to do a story on bullfighting for NPR, knowing the pariah reputation of this activity and the nature of our listening audience. (I once innocently mentioned in a story how President George H. W. Bush had switched from dove hunting to fishing to appease animal rights zealots. A hyperventilating listener e-mailed me, "And so you don't think fishing commits violence on the fish?!")

I sold the bullfighting story to a magazine and asked my friend from Austin, photographer Will Van Overbeek, to come along. Martínez had agreed to a profile with two ground rules: no pictures with his girlfriend (his wife lived in Monterrey) and no shots of him holding his favorite beer, Coors (which would have angered his sponsor, Carta Blanca).

I pointed at the two bull heads on his wall and said I was from Texas and I'd been around rodeo bulls. "How are they different from brave bulls?" I asked.

"A regular bull will chase you and may even wound you. A brave bull, his mentality, the totality of this being, is made to kill you. You can't domesticate it. It is fierce," Martínez said, searching my face to see if I was an undercover antibullfighting activist.

On the wall opposite the great ruminant heads was a poster-size photo of Martínez at his first *despedida* on May 30, 1982, the afternoon that people thought was to be his retirement fight. The matches took place in the 50,000-seat Plaza Mexico, the largest bullring in the world. Martínez had fought there 91 times, more than any matador before or since; so many times that his public nicknamed it La Plaza de Manolo. The event was considered of such significance that it was broadcast live throughout the republic.

After much rummaging, he found a videotape and popped it into a VCR. A picture flickered on the screen of a large flower-trimmed sign that read "Adios Manolo." The commentator, Pepe Alameda, Mexico's Red Barber of the bullring, was frothing on about this "artist from Monterrey . . . his extraordinary rhythm . . . his complete domination . . ." We watched a younger Martínez in the arena, feet immobile, legs locked, back arched, straight as a pine tree, whipping the red cape over the bull's head again and again. He performed the passes with such precision and proximity that it reminded me of what the young matador had said—it's like he tells the bull what to do.

His last bull was roan with pearly horns and massive shoulders and neck, a creature that appeared to be made of pure muscle. With blood trickling from a lance wound and four barbed sticks in its back, he never lost his spirit. He charged furiously each time, searching the cape with his horns for the man he wanted to destroy. Though he panted and his tongue hung out, he attacked tirelessly again and again. He was magnificent.

After he killed the great bull, Martínez was rewarded with high honors: a *vuelta al ruedo* (victory lap around the ring) along with both ears and the tail. Distraught fans threw hats, roses, shoes, and jackets into the arena. We watched as his long-time manager, José Chafik, ritualistically cut off the matador's short ponytail—a Samsonian touch—signifying his retirement from the ring. When the videotape ended, no one spoke. The men were awkwardly aware of the brooding 45-year-old former matador splayed on his recliner, holding a Coors.

We all went to bed. Late that evening I heard the crazy driver, Antonio, in the living room watching tape after tape of Martínez's fights. On my way to the bathroom, I saw him standing on the cowhide rug before the television, mimicking his mentor's impeccable posture as he caped an invisible bull in a direct line from front to back.

❖

The Mexican bullfight is a highly structured and ritualized contest that adheres to the classic Spanish *corrida de toros*. It is an archaic drama of life and death that is not supposed to be fair or juried or politically correct. It is supposed to be beautiful and emotional.

In the opening *paseíllo*, the matadors and their assistants walk across the ring to stand in front of the judge's box while a band plays the traditional *paso doble*. On a typical program, three matadors each kill two bulls. The fight is divided into three acts, or *tercios*, each announced by a trumpet call. In the first, the bull is tested by men with magenta and yellow capes so that the matador can observe how his adversary charges. Then two picadors mounted on heavily padded horses jab lances called *varas* into the bull's neck and shoulders to test its ferocity and force it to lower its head so the matador can work it more easily. In the second phase, two banderilleros insert barbed sticks in the animal's shoulder area to correct any hook in its charge and energize it for the final stage.

In the climactic third act, *la faena*, the matador enters the ring alone with his *muleta* (red cape) to show what he is made of. The bull and the man should appear to work as a team. The matador coaxes the bull to pass as close to his body as possible, again and again, all the while exhibiting grace, artistry, skill, and valor. He should prove to the crowd his complete domination of the bull. Finally, the bullfighter takes the sword and plunges it into the animal, ideally piercing the heart and killing it instantly.

Bullfighting is a universe unto itself. There are said to be 42 terms just to describe the curvature of the horns. Entire dictionaries exist on the subject, from *abonado* (a spectator who buys season tickets) to *ventajista* (a show-off matador).

There is no American parallel to the position that a great matador holds in the Spanish-speaking psyche. North of the Rio Grande, a bull represents a vibrant stock market; south of the river, a bull means power and death. In Greek mythology, the supreme test of manhood is to slay a bull. The person who does, as Martínez did 2,943 times, achieves a degree of adulation that surpasses sports stardom. He becomes a shamanic warrior, something superhuman that has conquered death.

During his long career, which ended with his second and final retirement in 1990, Martínez had been *una figura*, a sensation. He fought on 1,345 afternoons, cut 1,500 ears and 189 tails, and took 220 vueltas. Six times he won the Golden Sword, the Heisman Trophy for Mexican matadors. No torero in the hemisphere remained on top for so long, fought more bulls, commanded a higher purse, received more accolades, won more devotees, or aroused more antagonists than Martínez. His fighting style—passionate, disciplined, artistic, serene—was so classic that it earned him his own noun: Martinismo. And his arrogant disdain of the clamor of the crowd created its own breed of detractors: los anti-Martinistas.

To understand what drove Martínez from the ring, you have to appreciate the peculiar nature of aficionados. Bullfighting is, at its heart, supremely populist. Unlike other sporting events that are refereed, judged, or scored by points, the accolade granted a successful matador at the end of an afternoon is largely the decision of the crowd. The bullfight judge presides over the orderly progression of the matches, but his decision to award the matador an ear is largely determined by the petitions of the spectators and the insistence of their fluttering handkerchiefs. Conversely, their hisses and boos, collectively known as *la bronca*, will often discourage the judge from giving anything to a matador who has displeased the public.

Aficionados have an opinion on everything. They want less lancing from the picador, more cape work from the matador, a better bull from the breeder, more bravura, less showboating, a slower kill, a quicker kill. The roar of a bullfight crowd reminds me of what spectators must have been like inside the ancient Roman Colosseum. The throng demands steadfast courage from both participants, man and beast, and punishes any show of fear. The *taxista* told me of witnessing an abdominal horn wound one afternoon after which the matador reached down, collected his intestines in his arms, and calmly walked out of the ring toward the surgeon. The people wildly applauded this show of bravery.

In order for a matador to become a sensation, he must cultivate his fans. "The people generally want the torero to do what the people want," said Julio Rivera, a craggy-faced, retired minor bullfighter employed by Martínez. "And many toreros did it. But Manolo never did. He had his own way. He was defiant. He never cringed before the people who tried to whistle him down."

"Manolo had a lot of power—over the crowd, over the bull, and over the other bullfighters," said Guillermo Cantú, regarded as Martínez's best biographer. "If you have a lot of power, you're like a dictator, and some people don't like you. A lot of people didn't like Manolo."

"Manolo was the last celebrity bullfighter," explained Adolfo Aguilar Zinser, the late Mexican United Nations ambassador and a loyal Martinista. "Everyone knew Manolo Martínez. His style was elegant, refined, classical. It was like watching a great dancer, like watching Isadora Duncan. As you become famous, you generate animosity. This is the dynamic of the plaza. The plaza can be like a monster."

Eventually, the plaza became a monster for Martínez. In the early 1980s, he began to put on weight, and his passes lost some of their elegance. Anti-Martinistas jeered and cajoled him relentlessly;

Martinistas demanded the old inspiration. "The people wanted more and more and more," said a close friend. "They would have stopped only when the bull gored him to death." On that afternoon in 1982 in the Plaza Mexico, Martínez hung up his suit of lights, he thought, forever.

One morning at breakfast at the ranch, I asked Martínez why he quit. "The public was always complaining. I was tired and bored. I said, 'I'm sick of this. I'm going to rest,'" he said. "I retired very young. I was only 35. I shouldn't have retired."

He moved to Brownsville, Texas, to enjoy the leisure life of a multimillionaire sports celebrity, but his retirement didn't last long. Like the bulls, Martínez was born to fight. So in 1987, four years and nine months after he left the plaza, he returned. Though he immediately received top billing at the best bullrings in the country, he encountered more of the same reaction. The crowd picked him apart with even more savagery because he was easier to criticize. He was older. He was heavier. What's more, his drinking and the fast life of a top-flight matador had begun to aggravate a stomach ulcer.

In March 1990, Martínez was scheduled to fight two bulls in Aguascalientes, but he never made it. "I felt very bad that day, and I went to the hospital," he remembered. "The doctor said one more fight would kill me. That was it.

"It's been two years," he said, with no bitterness. "I don't miss it anymore. Now I'm making my own *novilladas* [novice bullfights]. Everything changes with the years."

The calm of daybreak on Rancho Guadalupe was disturbed by a huge flock of great-tailed grackles that sounded like a thousand car alarms blaring at once. Martínez drove Will and me in his pickup toward his corrals to show us his favorite seed bull. As dawn awakened the landscape, I could see that it was beautiful and harsh: the prickly pear cacti, Joshua trees, and Spanish dagger all possessed sharp defenses, as did the *toros bravos* that roamed here.

It had rained overnight, making the road a muddy slurry that swallowed the pickup to its bumpers. Ranchhands had arrived in a tractor and were trying to attach a cable to the truck's undercarriage.

"*Cabrones! Pendejos!* Hurry up!" yelled Martínez, of whom it was said he dominated people the way he did bulls. Six miles and two mud-holes later, the Chevy Silverado stopped, and a vaquero jumped out of the back to open the gate. Martínez pulled into a corral that smelled of mud and urine and cut the engine. A dark form watched us from the corner. Its hide was as black as the wings of a grackle, though not shiny. Its muzzle was wet and its eyes alert. The half-ton bull was like some-thing Jurassic, a prehuman life form at the top of its food chain. The vaquero closed the gate and scrambled back into the pickup while the beast watched him intently, as if making some calculation. This bull was special. He had sired a champion that fought so fearlessly that a judge had, according to the rules of the plaza, ordered his life spared so his noble bloodline could be continued. The honor is known as an *indulto*.

"This is the father of the bull *indultado* in the plaza in Guadala-jara," Martínez said reverentially. "He's a *cabron*, no? He isn't any good anymore to mount; we use him only to take out the semen. But he's a great bull. He's beautiful. He's extraordinary," he said with a gaze most men reserve for women.

I asked if the old stud was still brave. Martínez shot me an incred-ulous look. "You can never take out the bravura. The character is inside them. All a breeder can do is form the physical."

Fighting bulls are distinguished from beef bulls by their distinc-tive forward-curving horns and the *morillo*, the hump of tossing muscle behind the head. Martínez once drove into the corral when two bulls were quarreling; both animals charged his pickup and drove a horn through the doors like they were soda cans. It is said that a Spanish bull once attacked a moving locomotive. "The bravery of a truly brave bull is something unearthly and unbelievable," wrote Ernest Hemingway in his classic 1932 treatise on bullfighting, *Death in the Afternoon.*

Hemingway said a fighting bull and a domestic bull are as different as a wolf and a house dog. Fighting bulls are the only type that will fight each other to the death. The breeder's challenge is to preserve the innate wildness and willingness to charge over and over at anything that moves, oblivious to pain. The best fighting bulls grow up in large, remote pastures where human contact is minimal. They are approached only in a vehicle or on a horse, never on foot, and never, ever with a cape. Bulls are intelligent. They learn quickly. The arena should be the animal's first experience with a man on foot.

The black sire, wary and implacable, stood across the corral watching us. Did it ever bother him, I asked, to raise these magnificent animals for four years, only to send them to their death for 15 minutes of entertainment?

Martínez's face tightened, and he drilled me with his dark, taurine eyes. "No," he answered curtly, "they are born for this."

I realized at that moment that I had stumbled into the Great Debate.

Ever since my first bullfight in the Plaza Mexico, I had never resolved my misgivings about the death of the bulls. It was not a doubt rooted in the ethic of animal rights; rather, I had trouble accepting the premise that the greater the bull's valor, the more the crowd savored the ritual of its killing—except for the few *indultos.*

Martínez sensed this in me and did not trust me. But on some level, I think we both accepted that the bull was the more honorable contestant. After a long career in the cutthroat business of bullfighting, Martínez had, late in life, come to trust only the bulls. He understood that matadors were vainglorious and overpaid, but the bulls, true to their breed, were pure and brave and lethal. He said as much to me: "The bull is more noble than many people. His eyes say that he is about to charge you, that he wants to kill you. Humans will not look you in the eyes before they betray you."

The *fiesta brava* was never intended to be a fair fight. It is a tragic drama that almost always ends in death, though rarely, these days, in the case of the bullfighter. The quality of trauma surgeons present at the bullrings has improved dramatically over the years. Nevertheless, it is the constant possibility of death to the matador that gives bullfighting its essence. It is the only spectacle—never call bullfighting a sport to an aficionado—that I can think of where a performer is expected to create art in the face of death, like a ballerina dancing in a minefield. And yet, bullfighting is everything its critics claim: barbarous, one-sided, and ultimately indefensible. At the end of many failed explanations of bullfighting, I have learned it's best not to bring it up in polite company.

The antibullfighting movement has gained momentum throughout Spain and Latin America in recent years, despite the abolition of one of the fiesta's most gruesome aspects. The bull used to maul the picadors' horses in front of the crowd, and many horses died a bloody death on the sand. Today the horses' undersides are protected by thick, quilted pads, but bullfighting opponents are undeterred. They denounce what they say are atrocities the crowds never see: bulls' eyes smeared with boot wax and kidneys beaten with sandbags to tilt the contest even more to the matador, horn tips sawed and sanded, vocal cords of horses slit to prevent their terrified bawling. Knowledgable aficionados

I have spoken with regard such abuses as scandalous and rare but undeniable.

Martínez was defiant. He pointed out that fighting bulls live more than twice as long as beef cattle. A *toro bravo* has a pampered life in a large pasture, after which he is killed swiftly, with dignity, whereupon the meat is butchered and sold to the public. In comparison, a beef steer lives part of its life in a cramped feedlot, is forced terrified into a slaughterhouse, and is dispatched by a bolt through the brain. "Which animal lives a better life?" he snapped.

Martínez tired of the conversation as he backed his truck out of the muddy corral. "The ecologists want to protect every living thing from rats to cattle. They are more pious than the pope," he said with finality.

A small bullring at Rancho Guadalupe had been freshly white-washed for the autumnal tradition known as *la tienta*—the test. Ten young cows were to prove whether they possessed the traits to mother brave bulls. They are judged on qualities that mock traditional animal husbandry. Wildness and aggressiveness are virtues. A cow should be quick to charge and eager to charge again. She should run straight and hold her head low. And she should attack the horse with great force, indifferent to the painful jabs of the lance. *Vacas bravas* that pass the *tienta* are sent back to pasture to join the harem of the seed bull. Those who fail are trucked to the slaughterhouse in Ciudad Victoria that afternoon.

Martínez sat above the ring in khaki slacks and a crisp blue shirt. The blue outline of the Sierra Madre Oriental rose up behind us, and the grackles had begun to caucus again. As each cow scrambled into the ring, a ranch hand called out her name, and Martínez wrote it in a notebook, then watched her intently.

Tientas give aspiring matadors a rare chance to practice with live animals. Under normal circumstances, a beginner recruits a friend to mimic the charging bull with a pair of mounted horns. "It's very hard to hold the horns and charge like a bull, and it's bad on your back," a *novillero* (novice bullfighter) told me.

Martínez made it a practice to encourage young bullfighters because he knew how hard it was to get started. His parents disapproved of the bullring. His father, a prominent Monterrey engineer, and his mother, the grandniece of the revolutionary hero Venustiano Carranza, wanted their son to be a professional, anything but a killer of bulls. It was dangerous. It was declassé. He went on to become the greatest toreador of his generation against the wishes of his respectable family.

On this sunny morning, he had invited the three *novilleros* who drove us to the ranch to test his cows. It was a great honor. Being asked to cape for Manolo Martínez was like a punk basketball player being invited to shoot hoops with Michael Jordan.

The ranch hands spread out around the ring, resting their forearms on the top rail, as the young men took turns with the red cloth. Martínez barked out corrections from his spot in the bleachers. "Close your legs up . . . Talk to her, *chingao* . . . You're fighting like you're looking in a mirror, *pendejo* . . . Softly, softly, let her come to the cape . . . Good, now on the left side." As the awkward young bullfighters tried to control the horned cows with simultaneous grace and fearlessness, I realized how easy Martínez had made it look.

By the end of the afternoon, the young men—covered with sweat and dust—gulped orange soda. Martínez was pleased that only two cows were dispatched to the butcher. Eight were to be bred with the bulls, and who knows, he said, one of their sons could grow up to be "as big as a cathedral and *indultado* in the Plaza Mexico."

❖

The day after *la tienta*, we all drove to Monterrey to watch three of Martínez's *novillos*, three-year-old bulls, perform in a bullfight. Only four-year-old bulls are allowed to go against full matadors; younger bulls are matched against *novilleros*. Evening found us in a restaurant called El Rey del Cabrito that served the local specialty of kid goat. The windowed roasting room displayed dozens of flayed goat carcasses slowly cooking over coals. Patrons turned and stared when the legendary matador entered the dining room. On the wall was a signed photograph of Martínez wearing his elaborate *traje de luces* and bushy seventies sideburns. A white-liveried waiter led us to a choice table in the corner. "Maestro, it has been a long absence," he said.

An elderly man with a drooping mustache approached our table with his head bowed, as though meeting a cardinal. "Matador," he said, barely audible, "would you be so kind as to sign my napkin?"

Martínez, petulant with his entourage, was magnanimous with his public. He still loved being *el mandon*, the godfather.

As he forked enormous helpings of goat into his mouth and pulled on a Carta Blanca—you have to keep the sponsors happy—I asked him how the *tienta* had gone. "Very well. Several of the cows were extraordinary," he replied.

"And the *novilleros*?"

"They were green. But within the green, they were good."

No one ever speaks of the danger of being a matador, though all professional toreros sooner or later feel the sharp, hot thrust of the horn. One morning at the ranch, Martínez's bathrobe slid open to reveal multiple scars crisscrossing the skin of his thighs, as though he had sat on a fragmentation grenade. He had been gored 15 times, 9 seriously, including the infamous 1974 attack of a bull named Borrachon—Drunkard—which almost killed him.

"Some gorings are triumphs," he said. "The people respect you because you wouldn't move; you were brave. If you are gored while running, it's a disgrace, no?"

The next day was a warm overcast Saturday. Martínez pulled his Ford Taurus ("pure coincidence," he insisted) up to an old stone-walled *plaza de toros* on the outskirts of Saltillo. As soon as he stepped out, men swarmed for autographs or just to clap him on the shoulder and call him Matador. Even when the handsome young *novilleros* arrived, strutting like peacocks in their skintight suits of light, Martínez was the king. Awestruck local reporters thrust tape recorders in his face, and he obligingly pontificated: "If you want to be a matador, you have to want it more than anything, more than eating, more than a woman."

The mammoth Cuauhtémoc Moctezuma brewery in Monterrey was putting on a series of *novilladas* across northern Mexico, and Martínez was the impresario in charge of booking the bulls and bullfighters. The old plaza was dominated by a 30-foot-tall inflated beer bottle. Inside, three babes in latex bicycle pants and tight Carta Blanca T-shirts sashayed around the ring. There seemed no limit to the brewery's resourcefulness; even bulls were named for beers—Bohemio, Tecato, and Indio. It seemed like crass commercialism to me, especially after Martínez's high praise for the animals' dignity, but he didn't seem to mind. Business was business.

As the afternoon wore on, the showstopper turned out to be a blond 23-year-old Spaniard named Manuel Díaz "El Cordobés," the illegitimate son of the famous Spanish matador of the same name. The son performed in the style of his father: slapping the bull's flanks; butting foreheads with it; and falling to his knees, daring it to charge him. At the end of the *faena*, when the sword was placed and the animal fell, Cordobés leaped into the air like a college cheerleader and landed on his knees. The crowd went nuts.

His flamboyant style was the antithesis of the sculpted, cerebral school of Martinismo. "He's risky," Martínez said, watching from behind the wooden *barrera*. "He's valiant but without art. He's a show-off just like his father was." But the impresario cannot be a purist, and by day's end Martínez was haggling with Cordobés's manager to book him again.

That night, we drove back to Monterrey to attend our last sporting event of the trip. Martínez had bought a bullring and named it Plaza Cuauhtémoc—for the brewery, not the Aztec chief. In a concession to public taste, the plaza alternated between bullfights and wrestling matches known as *lucha libre* (free fight) that were wildly popular among Mexican youths. Martínez sat in a folding chair in the stands holding a cup of beer. He wore the same expression of disgust he had when El Cordobés was fighting.

All around us, teenagers were shrieking in delight as two men histrionically pummeled each other with metal folding chairs inside the ring. That night's match pit Vampiro Casanova, a pouting, tattooed Canadian in dreadlocks, against El Fabuloso Blondy, a tubby, freckled Mexican who resembled Curly, the third Stooge. The evening climaxed when Vampiro leaned over the ropes and kissed a young female fan, setting off a squealing chant of "Vam-pir-o! Vam-pir-o!"

Just to rattle his cage, I asked Martínez how these wrestlers compared to bullfighters. "It is the difference between a housepainter and Picasso," he said, guffawing. Yet it was clear that many more youngsters were at the lucha libre than the bullfight.

"The bulls never have a chance. It's cruel and unfair," a teenage lucha libre fan told me at the snack stand.

I asked Martínez about the future of the fiesta de toros with a new generation that wasn't as interested in bulls as their fathers had been. He scoffed again: "Do you believe that Mexico will modernize so much that it will abandon the sexual act with a woman? It is the same with the bulls."

The aging matador stared without expression at the clowning, costumed figures inside his bullring. The screaming of adolescent girls drifted outside the arena and reached the darkened corrals where six bulls from Rancho Guadalupe moved about nervously, feinting at shadows.

Manolo Martínez died in 1996 at age 50 at a hospital in La Jolla, California, while awaiting a kidney transplant.

Chapter 10

THE HUMAN FARMER

T HE RAINS CAME and stayed. The rotating storm clouds stalled over Central America for eight days, producing as much as five feet of rain in some places. The ceaseless precipitation created flash mudslides that interred whole villages. Mountainsides melted and washed away. As the earth liquified, urban shanties slid down slopes and landed in splinters. The downpour was so relentless and destructive that some thought it was the end of the world.

Hurricane Mitch killed more than 5,600 people, left 2 million homeless, and changed the topographic map of Mesoamerica in the autumn of 1998. Honduras and Nicaragua, already among the poorest nations in the hemisphere, staggered under the natural disaster. Highways, bridges, schools, and water systems that governments could ill afford to repair would have to be entirely rebuilt.

I flew into Tegucigalpa, Honduras, three months later to report on the terrible aftermath of Mitch. There was little positive to say. Grieving peasants had lost family members. Refugees were angry about conditions in government shelters. Government ministers were overwhelmed. One day, a local employee for World Neighbors, an Oklahoma-based nongovernmental organization (NGO) that supports sustainable farming methods, told me about a buzz in the NGO community. Reports were trickling in that the plots of farmers who had used soil conservation techniques sustained less damage than those of traditional farmers.

Mitch may have been an act of God, but in certain areas the degree of destruction was manmade. As farmers watched their fields and pastures wash away, the mighty storm laid bare the folly of conventional agriculture. Deforestation and slash-and-burn cultivation had left hillsides vulnerable to erosion. It was harsh validation of what an eccentric and passionate agronomist had been preaching for years: You must change your ways. His name was Don José Elías Sánchez, and I was urged to visit his farm, Granja Loma Linda, for a glimpse of a revolution in agriculture.

Following my tipster's instructions, I drove up into the thickly forested Valle de Angeles on the outskirts of the capital. When I parked my rental car, Sánchez greeted me like an old friend and immediately invited me into his temporary home for a plate of pancakes, cooked by his wife, Candida. He was fit and vigorous at 71, wearing a plaid shirt and jeans. His smile was generous, his eyes wise and skeptical, and his deeply tanned skin had the luster of an old wallet.

"Mitch came with a full bladder," he said, chuckling.

The flood-swollen Rio Chiquito, normally a gentle brook that flows through his hillside farm, had burst an upstream dike, roared down the watercourse, and gouged an ugly gash 80 feet wide and deep enough to reveal bedrock. Worse, the torrent swept away every structure he had built. Sánchez pointed to a shelf of land beside the floodway where his house had stood.

"We have lost everything. Our house, the dormitory, our clothes, my library, all my photographs," he said sadly. But his smile quickly returned. "Everything except my garden."

While the flood devastated everything close to the streambed, the damage to the rest of his farm was minimal.

"Come and look," he said, bounding up a hillside, a machete swinging at his side. Cicadas buzzed like an electric circuit in the midday

rolling explorers to discover new spice routes to the Far East. There were hundreds of programs, many proclaiming they had discovered the key to saving rural economies. Rural folk were collecting fallen butterfly wings in the forest and selling them in gringo boutiques. Why not? The more touchy-feely they sounded, the more money they collected from funders, and the more stories they generated from softhearted journalists. With microphone and Immodium in hand, I headed south to visit some of these efforts to see how conservation and capitalism were coexisting.

There was shade-grown coffee that provided bird habitat, loggers who hauled out fallen timber in oxcarts instead of forest-flattening trucks, community-owned ecotourism lodges that offered peasants an alternative to timber cutting, and harvesters who collected forest detritus and sold it as potpourri.

The only true success story I came across was the village of Ostional, on Costa Rica's lush Pacific coast. There, the townsfolk protect the endangered olive ridley sea turtle in exchange for the right to harvest its valuable eggs, considered an aphrodisiac by locals. I discovered that the turtle population was doing fine, but the people were at each others' throats. The project had grown so lucrative that the community was riven by avarice, jealousy, and scientific rivalry. All this so macho bar patrons could suck down the contents of the Ping-Pong ball–sized eggs with a beer and proclaim, as a bus driver told me, "Mmmmmm, they're delicious and nutritious, and they make a man more excitable!"

At the time, I, too, believed in the promise and exoticism of these rural innovations. Many of my radio stories glowed with the expectation that salvation was just around the corner if we would all keep the faith and keep trying. With eight years of hindsight, my focus has sharpened. During my investigations, I found lots of talent and good intentions, but the enterprises were rarely self-sustaining, and they usually depended on continuing contributions from foreign donors to stay afloat. The NGOs, swimming in foundation money, had bought new SUVs and assembled slick press packets; but in many cases, after a few years of disappointing results, funders contracted "donor fatigue," pulled the plug, and the project collapsed.

In the end, my idealism collided with the hard truth that conservation rarely pays its own way, that things worth protecting cannot necessarily be made profitable. Sometimes they simply have to be protected with boundaries and park rangers and government commitments. One of the few scientists willing to acknowledge this, at the time, was Kent Redford, then head of Conservation Science and Stewardship at the Nature Conservancy.

"The myth of sustainable development," he said with a sigh. "There's something about the human psyche that wants win-win solutions and cost-free approaches. I'm afraid we want to be deceived. The conservation community has clasped to its bosom the asp of sustainable development, and we're slowly dying as a result of it."

The Rosetta Stone many conservation groups seek is a way to stop slash-and-burn agriculture, a major cause of deforestation in the developing world. Campesinos move into a poorly protected forest reserve, fell trees, burn them, plant crops, and enjoy two or three years of good production. But the soil fertility that came from the rich forest detritus rapidly depletes; and because the farmers don't know how to improve the soil, after a few growing seasons, they move farther into the woods to repeat the slash-and-burn cycle. After the natural nutrients have disappeared, peasants sometimes sell these cleared lands to cattle ranchers, whose animals overgraze the pastures, thus contributing to soil destabilization and preventing forest regrowth.

But what if a farmer could learn how to keep his land fertile year after year? He could grow heartier crops, his family would be healthier and better off, and he wouldn't have to constantly seek new land or move off the land entirely to migrate to an urban slum or the United States. What was needed was an indigenous, homegrown solution to backward farming practices. I finally found it on Granja Loma Linda.

José Elías Sánchez was born in 1927 on a large farm in the southern province of Choluteca, Honduras, and quickly showed his intelligence and knack for innovative thinking. As a young college graduate, he rose quickly through the educational bureaucracy, where he was noticed by the US Agency for International Development and awarded a scholarship for a master's degree in educational administration at the University of New Mexico. His résumé lengthened. In 1969, he was appointed director of the Honduran National School of Agriculture and later assigned to the influential position of training all agriculture extension workers. By this time, he had already identified the basic concept that made his teaching so powerful and relevant to Honduran farmers.

"In tropical countries, all agronomists are trained to work in fertile valleys, in flat soils. In Honduras, 80 percent of the farmers live on hilly land. For this, we started Loma Linda," he told me.

Sánchez founded Granja Loma Linda, literally, Pretty Hillside Farm, in 1974 to prove to compesinos that inclined fields on marginal lands, though harder to farm, did not have to be unproductive. By 1989, there were so many farmers, extensionists, agronomists, and students trooping through Loma Linda to see the astonishing productivity for themselves that Sánchez quit his government job and accepted his calling as a master farmer and teacher. He envisioned the Granja to be the opposite of the government experimental station, with its top-down, expert-driven transfer of technology. Elias wanted his to be a simple farmer-to-farmer training center, with 90 percent of the time spent tromping through the crop rows and 10 percent in the classroom. By the time he finally moved to Loma Linda from his house in the capital in 1991, he had constructed dormitories, showers, a kitchen, classrooms, an office, and his own home overlooking the gentle Rio Chiquito. The teaching outreach at Loma Linda was supported by World Neighbors. Sánchez was ready to save the world—or at least his steep, nutrient-starved piece of it.

When groups of 25 to 30 students came for weeklong seminars at Loma Linda, they were greeted in the classroom by a poster of a white pig wearing dark glasses and lying in a hammock. "In my farm, there are two leaders," Don Elías told them. "I am one and the pig is the other. You cannot follow both. I wake at 4 a.m. and the pig sleeps all day. Who will you follow?"

Sánchez was unable to see how there could be improvement in a farm without concomitant progress in the condition of the farmer. He ordered his students to wash their hands before meals and change their underwear every day. He inveighed against machismo and drunkenness.

"He emphasized that whatever activity a person learns is an internal change. Each one of us is a human farm, with a mental ability and conscience to work for ourselves, our communities, and nature, of which we're a part. This was a very powerful idea for me," said his longtime colleague Milton Flores-Barahona.

Sánchez was a natural teacher. He used aphorisms the way Jesus used parables. Many of them are collected in an illuminating, affectionate book, *The Human Farm, a Tale of Changing Lives & Changing Lands*, by Katie Smith Milway.

- If the mind of a campesino is a desert, his farm will look like a desert.
- The environmental degradation of the campesinos' farms is only another expression of the personal and spiritual degradation of those who work the land.
- Weed your hearts.
- When Americans come here and see misery, they have a bleeding heart and they give things away. I'm not going to give anything away.

Sánchez saved special venom for government-schooled agronomists whose reliance on agrochemicals he mocked. At meals, he often sat with the farmers and spurned the extensionists. By the end of his life, he had many antagonists in the formal agriculture schools, which troubled him not one whit.

"Agronomists are a plague," he said. "They strut around with their equipment and their answers, stepping on plants and people as they go."

Don Elías was part of a quiet, grassroots rebellion to the Green Revolution that swept the globe in the 1940s, '50s, and '60s. The touchstones of the Green Revolution are hybrid seeds, monocropping, irrigation, tractors, chemical fertilizers, pesticides, and herbicides. But Sánchez doubted their applicability to the subsistence farmers of mountainous Honduras. Chemical inputs are more expensive than the average farmer can afford, and when the chemicals are misused, they can harm both the peasant and the soil. What's more, this agricultural paradigm favored big farmers who had all the arable bottom land and could afford a tractor and hybrid seeds. Sánchez wanted to teach Honduran growers how to get the most out of their meager, upland plots. But first there were lessons they had to unlearn.

The one-room, adobe houses with their red tile roofs that look so quaint from rural highways are at the center of what social scientists call "extreme structural poverty." Honduras is one of the poorest countries in Latin America and the Caribbean. According to a 2005 report by the International Food Policy Research Institute, two out of every three Hondurans is poor, with a per capita income of less than a dollar and a half a day. Child mortality is 32 per 1,000 births and more than three-quarters of the population is illiterate. Poverty figures spike even higher in rural, hillside areas—the zones Don Elías targeted—where more than 90 percent of the population lives on less than a dollar a day. Here, families live in a daily struggle to raise enough maize and beans to stave off hunger.

With Sánchez's long association with Honduran farmers, he knew their backward practices all too well. Campesinos generally don't know how to keep their children or their soil healthy, and their lives turn into a lifelong downward spiral, a race against human disease and depleted soil. The whole grim enterprise is exacerbated by Catholic fatalism—they suffer on earth because the rewards in heaven are great. The inability to raise adequate healthy crops creates its own ripple effects of despair. Poor families that have eight children or more are assured that none is fully fed. The failure of subsistence can create pressure on the breadwinner to take seasonal labor in distant coffee and sugarcane plantations, where living conditions are even worse.

Sánchez's fundamental challenge was to bind the soil to the hillside. He did this through terracing and digging contour ditches to catch and channel rainwater, but he had a distinctive twist on this ancient method of soil conservation. He reasoned, why till land where you're not going to plant? The classic technique he pioneered was *branza minima*, known as minimum or in-row tillage, in which only the area around the food plant is cultivated and the spaces between plants are left untilled. In order to protect them from washouts, the farmer allows weeds to grow in the unneeded spaces, or he lays old corn stalks in them that can be later used for compost. The place where the corn or bean or squash plant is growing is built up as a "microterrace" that stops the water and creates an efficient, fertile growing space.

Sánchez taught his students how to make their own fertilizer in the form of compost heaps of corn stalks, animal manure, and kitchen waste. He was also a fan of cover crops, such as velvet beans or clover, that prevent soil erosion, crowd out weeds, hold in moisture, and fix nitrogen in the soil. They were simple, inexpensive methods adapted to local needs on marginal farmlands. His genius was to show farmers how to get more yield from less land.

"What he was successful in doing with farmers was to get them to realize all kinds of potential they never dreamed of. He was growing maize on Loma Linda they had never imagined was possible. He inspired farmers, shocked them into realizing if they did a few things differently, they could be better off," said Roland Bunch, a Tegucigalpa-based expert on agricultural sustainability and himself a legend in Central American agroecology.

Since Sánchez's death from a heart attack on March 18, 2000, his widow, Candida, now watches over Granja Loma Linda. But the work he did promoting sustainable farming is now largely carried on by his students, which he estimated at more than 20,000 in the quarter century during which he taught. The same hard question must now be asked of his legacy that I asked of the sustainable development projects. How much of a difference did he make?

It would be wonderful to end this chapter with the observation that the teachings of José Elías Sánchez are revolutionizing agriculture in Central America, but it's not that simple. The problems are structural and age-old. His influence has been subtle but palpable.

The Rural Development Project of Lempira Sur, supported by the United Nations Organization for Agriculture and Food, found in 2005 that in municipalities where Sánchez's human farming teachings were applied, the poverty level fell 14 points lower than the rest of the province. Not a dramatic improvement, but measurable nonetheless.

"Don Elías was not a technician; he was a teacher and as such he taught work habits so the people could transform themselves," said Luís Alvarez Welchez, a Sánchez alum and director of the UN's Lempira Sur project.

His impact is perhaps strongest in two teaching centers in Central America: the Agricultural School of Humid Tropical Regions in Costa Rica and the Panamerican Agriculture School in Zamorano, Honduras, founded by the United Fruit Company. The renowned agricultural institute known simply as Zamorano used to be the embodiment of the Green Revolution, and its faculty were frequent objects of Sánchez's derision. Unlike many similar state-supported schools throughout Central America, however, Zamorano recognized and accepted the gospel according to Don Elías.

"Elias was right about many things, especially about the hubris and lack of commitment of many agronomists, the damage caused by certain agricultural technologies, and the incompleteness of traditional extension approaches. Because of people like him, we in Zamorano had to rethink our assumptions and redesign our programs," said Dr. Keith Andrews, who worked at Zamorano for 22 years, the last nine as director.

The human farm has had a profound influence on the NGO World Neighbors as it continues to work in Central America searching for solutions to hunger, poverty, disease, and promoting a healthy environment. One day, a World Neighbors extensionist took me northeast of Tegucigalpa to meet one of its farmer/teachers. We drove along dirt roads through cattle pastures that had once been hardwood forests. Every tiny *tienda* we stopped in for cold Cokes had a lighted candle to Nuestra Senora de Suyapa, the patron saint of Honduras. At midafternoon, we pulled into the ragged village of El Pie de la Cuesta, which means "the foot of the hill," and hiked up to Manuel Herrera's hillside farm.

"Buenas tardes," said Herrera, who looked to be in his fifties, with white whiskers, a tattered shirt, rubber boots, and a machete. Three of his eight children were playing with broken toy cars on the hard-packed ground outside his adobe house. His wife peered at us from the smoky interior.

Don Manuel had been a typical corn farmer until the NGO singled out his farm to serve as a model to show his neighbors some different growing techniques. With lithe steps, he led us up into his fields to show how he was growing velvet beans to fix nitrogen and planting vertiver grass to avoid erosion. He had cultivated banana trees, onions, carrots, and soybeans—which may sound like basic crops but are an innovation in this part of Honduras. When we got to his corn, he beamed at the tall, healthy plants, the result of in-row tillage and compost amended with material from his own outhouse.

"My neighbors, too, have noticed that my corn is better. Thirteen of them have come to see," he said. "But they know the work is harder. You can't just plant and leave it, as in the past, or burn and move on. You have to dedicate time to it."

I knew then that Don Manuel had planted corn in his mind before he had planted it in the earth.

Chapter 11

THE LEAF PLAYER
OF MEXICO CITY

AT FIRST, I THOUGHT the strange sound emanating from the portico just off the *zocalo* was a vendor selling a bird call. But the closer I got, the more it sounded like music. Was it a harmonica or the high notes from a crazy violin? I crossed the street and followed the piercing, mellifluous notes to the stone walkway in front of a state government office. There, sitting cross-legged on the sidewalk, was a one-armed man holding to his upper lip what appeared to be a leaf.

"Carlos Garcia, *a sus órdenes*," he said when I introduced myself.

The 71-year-old man with gentle, weary eyes sat on a denim cushion on the sidewalk with his huarache sandals crossed in front of him. The sleeve of his faded blue work shirt was knotted where his right arm should have been. An upturned straw hat beckoned pesos.

The amazing sound he produced came from blowing against a sprig of variegated English ivy so that the leaf edge vibrated against his lower lip. It was a sound that kids make by blowing on a blade of grass, but Garcia had elevated it to artistry. He was playing ground cover with expressiveness, intonation, and vibrato.

I started calling out old tunes—"Adelita," "Jalisco"—and he knew them all.

"One time Televisa filmed me," he said. "The announcer said,

'Here we have Carlos Garcia with his musical leaf.' That's what they called it, the musical leaf. I call it *la melodia*."

I was late for an interview with a labor activist to hear about the mistreatment of workers at a Korean-owned garment factory in Puebla. That was the story I had come to report in May 2001. But at that moment, I realized the invisible hands of the radio gods had brought me to Carlos Garcia. I sat down next to him on the sidewalk. A policeman getting his black boots polished nearby watched the two of us impassively—the gringo with the microphone and the *viejito* with one arm.

Garcia explained that he had been supporting himself and his family for more than 40 years on the tips he earned from his street music. "God gave me the ability to do this, because not everyone can do it," he said enthusiastically. "The people who pass by here inspire me. They say, 'How marvelous! How pretty you play!' "

Garcia belonged to the millions in Mexico City who take part in what social scientists call the urban informal economy. Some sell cheap watches on the street, others pick recyclable garbage from the city's mountainous dump, some blow fire in clown face at stoplights, and some make music on the sidewalks. There are Aztec flutists, organ grinders, mariachis, marimbists, violinists, and Garcia.

He learned to toot on a leaf as a boy growing up on his father's dryland farm, Rancho Valenciano, in the municipality of Ixtlan de los Hervores in the state of Michoacan. As the uneducated son of a poor campesino family with nine children, he knew no one who could afford a real music instrument like a guitar or a trumpet. Kids picked leaves and tried to shape the squeaky sound into recognizable tunes. In Ixtlan de los Hervores, several people could play the leaf, but Garcia surpassed them all. I wondered what, with his native musicality, he might have accomplished had he had access to a real instrument and a music teacher.

Garcia never intended to be a full-time leaf player, but his life took a cruel turn when he was 13. Disobeying his father, he touched a fallen live power line that burned his right arm so severely that the limb had to be amputated. After that, he did the only work available to a disabled and illiterate young man—he hired out as a field laborer, cutting weeds with his good arm. He and his siblings were on their own after their father sold the meager rancho. Garcia married and started his own family. By the time he was 30, he realized he could not support his wife and four daughters, so in 1959, like millions of other impoverished rural residents, he migrated from the countryside to the capital.

There, his musical hobby became his livelihood. He began playing in buses for tips and found that people were surprised and delighted by his music—much like I had been. "I made the decision not to ask the passengers for anything. I played my melodia, and they gave me what they wanted, and I thanked them," he said, as office workers hurried past us on their lunch hour.

He taught himself to read and write so he could follow the routes on the buses. He eventually found his regular spot in the cool shade beside the zocalo, where Aztec ruins, a Spanish colonial cathedral, and modern government buildings coexist.

Garcia had improvised a living. He said he occasionally encountered other leaf-blowing buskers on the sidewalks and subways of Mexico City, but no one was as good as him. He earned about $40 a week in tips, with which he raised four daughters and a son, bought a small house in an outlying barrio, and moved into Mexico's working class. This is not to say that Garcia was well-off or even comfortable, but his music earned him an income that elevated him above the abject poverty of other migrants who lived on hillsides in tin-roof shanties.

After we talked for about 45 minutes, I dropped a healthy tip in his hat, thanked him for his story, got his telephone number—yes, he had a phone—and said good-bye. At that moment, neither of us had any idea how famous he was about to become.

When I returned to Austin, I called my sister, a gifted piano teacher with perfect pitch, and played her some of his leaf music over the phone. "Elizabeth, is he any good?" I asked.

"He plays with feeling, he plays in tune, and he can hit a high B. He's pretty amazing," she said.

When my Puebla garment-workers story went on the air, it landed with a forgettable thud. But my feature on Carlos Garcia, the Leaf Player of the Zocalo, caused an uproar. NPR listeners loved him.

The most encouraging reaction came from Kronos Quartet, the brilliant, avant-garde string quartet that once arranged Jimi Hendrix's "Purple Haze" for strings. Their publicist told me the San Francisco–based group had been working for five years on a recording project about the musical traditions of Mexico, and they had been looking for Carlos Garcia. David Harrington, the group's artistic director and first violinist, had heard him on a trip to Mexico City in 1995. "It was so empowering to know that an object like a leaf can be turned into a musical instrument that's not a million-dollar Stradivarius," Harrington told me on the phone. "That experience changed the way I thought about instruments."

I drew a map of where Garcia sat in the zocalo and faxed it to their producer in California.

After the world-changing impact of 9/11, I forgot about the leaf blower until April 2002, when Kronos released its Mexico project, *Nuevo*, on the Nonesuch label. The recording is an astonishingly original compilation of Mexican composers, traditions, and styles from sidewalks and concert halls. Reviewers were particularly taken with track 5, the love ballad "Perfidia," composed by Chiapas native Alberto Dominguez and featuring Carlos Garcia on the musical leaf. Kronos had not actually recorded Garcia for the CD. The group used an existing recording of Mexico City street musicians called *Sinfonia Urbana* that included Garcia playing "Perfidia." The chatter of vendors can be plainly heard behind his lovely rendition of the sad melody, which Kronos enveloped in a lush string arrangement. It was so beautiful that tears welled up in my eyes the first time I heard it.

Harrington loved it, too. "It's like he's at Carnegie Hall being accompanied by 101 strings," he said.

A few months later, I called Garcia at his house in Mexico City and asked him what he thought of the recording. He said lots of people had come by to tell him about the CD and my story on NPR, but he had yet to hear either one. And there was something else, he said, his voice falling. No one ever paid him for his recording—not the Mexican record label that put out *Sinfonia Urbana*; not Kronos. His tone was beseeching. He regarded me as his only contact to this distant, wealthy world of the music business.

I called Harrington back and told him what Garcia had said. He was stunned. "We followed all the proper procedures one follows to sample and get a license to use another artist's recordings," he said. "We paid for something they stole. We got ripped off, too."

Perfidy.

A couple of weeks before Christmas 2002, I returned to Mexico City to visit Garcia for a follow-up story. I was still getting e-mails from listeners curious about the leaf man. When I walked into the zocalo, the first thing I saw was a fake Christmas tree three stories tall, and the first thing I heard were the thunderous peals of the bells in the great cathedral towers. The famous bells each have names, such as La Dona, La Castigada, and Juan Diego, and some weigh more than the

Volkswagen taxis darting across the square. Then I caught the bird-like call of the leaf coming from the portico. How many places, I wondered, can one hear the commingling of one of the world's smallest and world's largest instruments?

Garcia was in his regular spot in front of the state government building, sitting cross-legged on a sheet of cardboard. Expecting me, he had laundered his work shirt and brought a portable stereo. "Some North Americans came by here and told me I was very famous up there," he said, smiling broadly, "They said there's a nice CD that everybody has heard with a *conjunto* called Kronos."

He was eager to hear the recording, so I gave him a CD, and he inserted it into his machine. His eyes widened when he heard the gorgeous strings behind his leaf.

When it was over, he said, "If I had been there, I would have played louder. I could do better the next time." Then he paused and smiled. "But the recording is very good, very good. They enter on time when I'm playing *la melodia*, and they carry the rhythm of the accompaniment."

He played it again. He motioned for a regular patron, Yvonne, a stout woman in a magenta dress who worked for the state, to stop and listen.

"Yes, that's you, indisputably!" she said. "I congratulate you very much, *jefe*. This is a major accomplishment."

She looked at me and continued, "He deserves it. He's an excellent person, always very clean, always smiling. His music is beautiful. I'm enchanted by it. I listen to him in the afternoons, and he transports me to different dimensions. But mainly it's him who is beautiful. May God always bless him."

Garcia beamed. He played it again.

"*Caray*—how pretty," he said.

I asked him how it was that he never got paid for the original recording. He said some people came by several years ago and recorded him, but he received "*ni un peso.*" Garcia said he had many needs. His wife, for instance, was going blind from cataracts, and he needed $2,500 for the operation. "As I told you on the phone, here the rich look down on the poor. This is the not the first time this has happened to me. But I'm not angry," he said. When he began to wipe away tears with a knuckle, I realized he had thought about his exploitation a great deal. "More than anything, I feel sad because it's not right they treat the poor this way," he said.

Garcia's eyes dried and his spirits lifted when he played the song a fourth time. A young man with spiky hair, a black T-shirt, and a nose ring stopped to listen. He gave his name as Gibrán and said he was a vocalist for a local band called the Enemies of Motherhood. His warm smile and friendly eyes belied his punk demeanor. "This man makes me happy. With a leaf from a tree he can make music like this. It's incredible," he said with gusto.

Garcia heaved himself up on his left arm, then packed his things in a worn *mochila* with practiced one-handed dexterity. We walked out of the zocalo and descended a flight of stairs to the subway. Garcia walked briskly with the light, rolling gait of one who has memorized his route. He passed the man who sold *nopalitos* piled with shredded cheese, he passed the gravel-voiced hawker of soccer tabloids, and he stopped at a kiosk named Perfumeria Sisi. Behind the tiny counter was a middle-aged woman whose cherry-red lipstick matched the color of her apron and fruity perfume reeked like auto air freshener. Garcia appeared to be sweet on her. He hauled the boom box out, set it on a stack of boxes of Angel Face Powder, and played the song again.

After "Perfidia" ended, Sisi didn't seem sure how to respond. "That's your song?" she asked tentatively.

"They are los Kronos, very famous up there," he said casually, motioning north with a jut of his chin.

"It's very nice," she replied fondly.

I could see that his usual trip home would take longer on this special day. We rode the Number Two line from the zocalo to Pino Suárez, then transferred to the Number One line to Boulevard Aeropuerto. The subway corridors were crowded now with homebound workers clutching briefcases and lunch pails. We ascended a flight of stairs onto a sidewalk full of vendors, one of whom was Garcia's friend, José Cruz, the snack seller. Garcia pulled out the CD player and set it next to a display of salted pumpkin seeds and chocolate Santas. The secretaries, accountants, and security guards streaming up the stairs looked quizzically in the direction of the soaring violins, cello, and viola that seemed so out of place amid the din of the city.

"They are famous, los Kronos," Garcia said, adding out of nowhere, "They are millionaires."

The song ended. "That's it," he concluded, chuckling happily.

Cruz looked at his old customer with new admiration. Fumbling for words, he said, "It's very relaxing."

The final leg of Garcia's homeward journey began at the bus stop, where he introduced me to Daniel, the bus dispatcher. This time he pulled out only the CD paper insert and pointed to the credits. "Number five. Carlos Garcia. That's me," he said with an air of modest greatness. "The disc is very popular up there, and los Kronos is a very famous band."

"Mmm. How nice," said Daniel, nonplussed.

The driver of a green and white microbus hit his horn, which emitted a Tarzan yell, indicating that he was ready to leave. We took seats behind the driver, who had taped a picture of a bleeding Christ next to a sticker that read "Freaky Behavior." The micro pulled into the tide of afternoon traffic heading southeasterly out of the capital, toward the distant cone of a dormant volcano known as *La Mujer Dormida*, the Sleeping Woman. As we bounced along, young religious pilgrims on bicycles passed in the other direction on their way to la Basilica in honor of Our Lady of Guadalupe Day.

Forty minutes later, we were walking along an unpaved street through a *colonia* of cinderblock homes spray painted with gang graffiti. There were posters for a congressional candidate who promised "attention and responsiveness to citizens' complaints." Garcia ambled through the neighborhood, which to my radio-tuned ears emitted all the classic sounds of a Latin American barrio: barking dogs, calling roosters, crying babies, and blaring radios. Turning a corner, he suddenly stopped in front of a wall covered with strands of thick green ivy. "Here," he said, eyes twinkling, "are my instruments."

My follow-up story about Carlos Garcia's uncompensated fame generated an even greater response. A few listeners castigated Kronos for not ensuring he had been paid. One traveler suggested Garcia lodge a complaint with the World Intellectual Property Organization in Geneva.

Several listeners informed me that Mexico is not the only country where people make music from leaves. One traveler told me he had seen boys playing musical leaves in Poland and Slovakia. After I did more research, I learned that, indeed, there were accounts of foliar musicians all over the world: Quezon City, the Philippines; Hainan Island, China; Morgan County, Alabama; and even Henry David Thoreau's Walden Pond: "I remember well one gaunt Nimrod who would catch up a leaf by the roadside and play a strain on it wilder and more melodious, if my memory serves me, than any hunting-horn."

Most of the e-mails expressed a desire to donate money to the leaf man. Within days of the story, Kronos posted a message on its Web site that began, "We at Kronos are very dismayed to learn of Carlos's current situation" and announced the creation of the Carlos Garcia Fund. Delighted, I routed all the offers of donations to them. A few months later, I called Garcia, and he told me jubilantly that Kronos had sent him a check for $2,890.

In journalism, we call that a happy ending. The kid with cancer gets a trip to Sea World; the old lady's house is saved from the wrecking crew; Garcia's wife gets her eye operation. Journalists are thrilled when our stories bring about change. It makes us feel that we have accomplished something beyond professional voyeurism. We haven't just observed the world; we have in some small way helped to improve it. But the blinkered focus of a typical 30-inch or 7-minute news story does not fully represent the complexity of real life. Charity prompted by a poignant story rarely changes the thing that causes the problem. In Carlos Garcia's case, the immediate result may have been happy, but it wasn't the ending.

Two and a half years passed before I checked in with Garcia again. I wasn't sure he was even still alive, but he picked up the phone. *"Hola, Juanito. Como estas amigo?"*

I told him I was coming to Mexico City for another assignment and wanted to visit him at his home. He quickly jumped to the subject of money. The Kronos check was long gone, he said, and times were tough for him and his wife, Ramona. He gave me directions to his *colonia*, and we made plans to get together the following Friday.

The morning the taxi picked me up at my hotel, there was a protest taking place at the famous Angel of Independence monument. On each of the steps surrounding the Corinthian column on which stands the winged golden angel, a line of men stood with their underwear pulled down to reveal their bare bottoms. There must have been 300 of them. A stocky fellow in white briefs was yelling something into a bullhorn. As I learned later, they were campesinos from the state of Vera Cruz who were demanding an audience with the president to protest the unjust appropriation of their lands by a local politician. The protest had made the front pages on the first day, but by the time my taxi sped past El Angel, they had been there for three weeks, and the mass mooning had lost its shock value.

"*Que barbaro!*" my cab driver said, shaking his head. "Their asses are getting toasted in the sun."

I thought about the desperation that drives peasants like these to take such a drastic, outlandish tactic to achieve justice. I thought of Garcia fleeing Michoacan in the 1950s with his family and no employable skills to survive in the city. I wondered whether he was still making a living with his musical leaf.

After a long drive to the edge of the metropolis, we entered the same dirt-street neighborhood I had visited earlier and parked next to a small weed-choked park. His house was unmistakable, painted a bright avocado green and fronted by a tiny fenced rectangle of rosebushes and Alcatraz flowers. When Garcia came to the door, I immediately noticed he looked older and some of the brightness had drained from his eyes. There had been chilly rain showers all morning, and he was wearing a threadbare thermal vest.

"The *drogadictos* are out this morning," he said, casting an eye toward several sweatshirted figures in the sad little park.

We stepped into a cozy living room furnished with a pink couch and decorated with silk flowers and ceramic bric-a-brac animals.

"I have a desire to go to your country and play for the people," he said, "but I fear that I'm headed for the cemetery instead. I'm getting old and sick."

As if on cue, Garcia emitted a deep, phlegmatic cough and dabbed his mouth with a tissue. He said his 74-year-old wife's health was declining—bad kidneys, high blood pressure, and her cataracts were growing back. He said the check from Kronos had paid for the original eye operation, living expenses, and treatment of an injury he received in a mugging. In early 2004, some neighborhood thugs pushed him down and stole his tips. He had to see a doctor for an injured knee. He pulled up his trouser leg to show me the nasty scar and describe in gory detail how the doctor had cleaned out the infected wound. With a hurt knee, he hadn't been able to play in public for four months, so his daughter, Socorro, whose husband owns a small metalworking shop, had helped him out.

When the subject of his daughter came up, Garcia began to cry. He said on the first day of the year, his second daughter, Teresa, had died of kidney failure after she stopped responding to dialysis. "My mother and my father died, but you don't feel the same when your child dies," he said.

Finally, he said his church, the Jehovah's Witnesses, had expelled him because he had begun to drink again. "They don't talk to me. To my wife, yes, but not to me," he said unhappily. "We hope they'll reaccept me."

He brightened a bit when he brought out a notebook in which he had saved all the business cards of people who had contacted him since his appearance on the Kronos CD. There were reporters from the BBC, Reuters, Canal 11, and KHOU in Houston, as well as many well-wishers. But he complained that his fans couldn't find him now because construction had driven him out of his traditional spot in the zocalo. Now he was playing for tips in the subway.

"The trains push hot air before them, and it gets so hot down there," he said. "But I still enjoy playing the leaf. It's a blessing from

God Jehovah. He has given me this time because the Bible says our lives are 70 years, so I'm living an extra 5 years."

When I got up to leave, he presented me with a set of cassettes of sermons from his church, titled "Knowledge That Leads to Everlasting Life." I walked out the door of his green house and started to my cab. Looking for small talk, I asked about the shrine in the park that I assumed to be for the Virgin. "It is Santa Muerte," he said.

We walked over and stood before a pane of glass encasing a four-foot-tall, scary-looking fabricated skeleton dressed in a white robe and in whose bony hand someone had inserted a fat joint. Before her were set out cans of beer and saucers of pesos. A group of young men, loose-limbed, tattooed, and high, watched us from concrete benches. Garcia kept an eye on them. "This is *la virgin de los marijuaneros*," he said softly and bitterly. "They have taken over my neighborhood."

I told him I would see him the next day down in the subway, and I climbed into the cab for the drive back to my hotel.

I found Garcia at the entrance to the Boulevard Aeropuerto station. I bought a token and cleared the turnstile, and we made our way to the subway landing. A speedy train the color of ripe papaya whooshed to a stop, and we stepped aboard.

Subways are the same everywhere: No one makes eye contact, no one talks to one another, and everyone looks tired. As the moving car rocked back and forth, Garcia braced himself against a stainless steel support beneath the smiling picture of a gubernatorial candidate. He pulled a triangular leaf from his breast pocket and brought it to his lips. The sound was shrill and loud within the confines of the subway train, which lacked the pleasing acoustics of the stone walkway of the zocalo. A passenger reading a tabloid with a huge headline about "4 Cadaveres" pulled the newspaper higher to block his view of the subway busker. Another man put his fingers in his ears in irritation.

A woman dropped a few coins in Garcia's apron without looking at him.

We disembarked at the San Lazaro station, and he held up about 20 cents in change with a shrug of his shoulders. "I really want to go to the United States and play for your audience there," he said again with a suggestive smile. I had nothing encouraging to say, but I lied and said I'd look into it.

We stood awkwardly in the hot subway tunnel beneath the most populous city in the world as he waited for the next train. He hoped to make $10 to call it a successful night. I was about to spend twice that on dinner. After we said good-bye, I walked away and heard Garcia hock and spit loudly on the landing. I turned to watch him as he boarded the Linea Rosa train, and I wondered if I would ever see him or hear his musical leaf again.

EPILOGUE

ON LABOR DAY, a week after Hurricane Katrina struck, New Orleans has turned into Copville. The city is filled with national guardsmen, federal agents, state troopers, border patrolmen, wildlife rangers, and police officers from across the nation. They're heavily armed and paranoid and glowering at anyone not in a uniform. With exquisite understatement, NPR producer Anne Hawke says, "There's a lot of male energy in the city right now."

Fresh-faced guardsmen with M-16s at the ready march down Tchoupitoulas Street near my old haunt, Frankie and Johnny's. Guardsmen stand watch in front of the looted Brooks Brothers on Canal Street. Other guardsmen have "secured" the Audubon Zoo. We see sandbagged machine-gun emplacements on the green lawn in front of the entrance gates. Who, exactly, are they prepared to repel—a mob of looters storming the World of Primates to barbecue the gibbons?

It gets weirder.

A pickup drives around downtown, full of people wearing yellow T-shirts emblazoned with "Scientology Volunteer Minister" and handing out strange booklets titled *The Way to Happiness*.

Across the river in Jefferson Parish, which had less storm damage than Orleans Parish, some residents have already begun repairing their houses—if they can find a contractor. "Right now, if you gimme two Bourbon Street strippers and a roofer," says a wag at a Gretna café, "I'll keep the roofer."

The masses at the convention center are gone. What's left behind looks like a uniquely American refugee camp. I peer through the windows of the padlocked halls into a sea of empty packages on the foul carpet: Microwave Zesty Barbecue Meal, Ocean Spray cranberry juice, Kraft marshmallows, Lay's Classic Potato Chips, Planters peanuts, Tropicana orange juice, Kellogg's Corn Flakes, Nestea, Cheez-Its, Hawaiian Punch, Otis Spunkmeyer brownies. Consumer loyalty survives even in the darkest of times. There are thousands of empty wine and liquor bottles and, everywhere, old shoes and used clothing that were discarded when the refugees went shopping.

Someone has written graffiti on the outside wall: "Everybody in this bitch stay cool. God bless the dead. We will not get fuck [sic] over by the killers 'n' da law."

The media are in full descent. The *Sydney Morning Herald* is at the Audubon Zoo, shooting a picture of the kookaburra that survived. Diane Sawyer is in the Lower Ninth Ward in a pressed white blouse and smart rubber boots. A reporter for Al-Jazeera Television is in Johnny White's Sports Bar in the French Quarter.

"In the Middle East we have sandstorms, the occasional stampedes at Mecca, but nothing like this," he tells me between sips of Abita beer.

Because the city has no power or water, there's no hotel designated as the official media beehive. Instead, news companies have brought in fleets of recreational vehicles that they park on the streetcar tracks on Canal Street, between toppled palms. It looks like an RVers' convention: Four Winds, Allegro, Sun Voyager, Sunseeker, Fleetwood Excursion.

NPR is there, too. Marty Kurcias—the go-anywhere, do-anything audio engineer who's parachuted into wars around the globe—has driven a 30-foot-long Majestic RV down from Washington. It's packed with extra batteries, minidiscs, sound cords, trail mix, canned peaches, cold beer, Gatorade, peanut butter, and a case of tuna fish (which we feed to abandoned cats).

Officer French says into his radio, "Seventeen twenty-two Franklin Avenue, twenty-nine on top of a vehicle. It's an unclassified death."

We push forward through the stinking black water onto St. Roche Street, and the officers spot two men on the second-story balcony of a stucco house. They smoke hand-rolled cigarettes and watch the lawmen warily. A third emerges from the fetid, waist-deep water and climbs the steps to the balcony.

"If you don't get treated from being in the water, you will die. You will die, sir," French yells up at them.

The men sit and smoke and watch us. They all appear to be high. "I want to go to my sister's in Atlanta; that's what I'm hoping," says one.

"This is the deal, guys—the water might be here for 80 more days, and they might call off rescue in the next day or two," French continues.

Another boat, this one full of Border Patrol agents in green uniforms, has floated up, and they second the policeman's entreaties. "Any significance to you stayin' there?" an agent asks wearily.

"We want to be here for our moms," says one of the men, without further explanation.

Hannigan groans. "Well, Mom ain't on an airboat," he shouts. "She ain't comin' here."

The trio has no intention of leaving. Dusk is falling, and nobody wants to be out after dark on these lawless canals with floating bodies. The boatman guns the engine, and we ease out of District Five. The officers deftly hold up electric lines so we can pass under them.

"I bet there are warrants out on those guys, and they don't want to go with cops. This is a huge drug haven—shootings every night," French says.

Hannigan shakes his head and adds, "All you can do is pray for the ones that decided to stay. They have their own reasons."

The postman pulls his airboat onto the trailer. French and Hannigan hop onto the ramp. "Why did so many New Orleans police desert after the storm?" I ask them.

"You gotta remember, these officers who turned in their badges—a lot of them lost everything," French says. "Their families said, 'I'm not coming back; I can't deal with this.' The stress—I've never seen anything like it. I can compare it to a living hell. I wouldn't and couldn't go through this again, but I stuck it out because I felt I had to be there for my fellow officers and the city. That's what I took an oath to do."

That night, we cook spaghetti on the propane range in the RV, and I write my story at the little folding table. At 3:00 a.m., we wake up Kurcias, and he sets up the sat phone outside on the sidewalk. With no time for an edit, we call Record Central, and the editor listens to the story as I'm filing. The mixer has one hour to produce a nine-minute story before *Morning Edition* goes on the air. This is called pushing deadline.

It's impossible to sleep after the adrenaline rush of a tight deadline, so I grab a beer and lay down on a blanket in the bed of my pickup. The boulevard is silent, and I admire the shining stars in the sky over the darkened city. The enormous and garish Harrah's casino—bitterly opposed by city preservationists when it was built—looms unlit to my left. On my right, young guardsmen on night watch sit in front of a looted shopping mall, cussing and smoking. They probably don't realize that they're part of the first military occupation of New Orleans since federal troops marched out of the city in 1877 after Reconstruction.

Fatigue creeps in, and the mind drifts. All week I've had a hard time remembering this is one of America's great cities. I expected to see refugees living in squalor in Honduras. I expected to see looters roam the streets of Baghdad. I expected martial law in Kosovo. How can this be happening in my own country?

And how is it that I'm here? After being a reporter for 26 years, I'm still not accustomed to parachuting into other people's grief: An Afghan girl beaten by the Taliban. An Albanian woman raped by Serbs. A Texas prison inmate waiting to die. An aged Mexican street musician climbing onto a subway for 45 cents in tips. I have a permanent case of survivor's guilt.

The whole Katrina disaster has been a hellish episode of *Survivor*. The setting is postdiluvian New Orleans. But it wasn't the death and dying that was so terrifying; it was the vision of society stripped bare and left to fend for itself. It was a candid camera on the soul. It was the ageless story of ourselves, with all our courage and corruption. And like a crew member on a reality series, I got to leave at quitting time. I could walk off camera, get in my truck, and drive to Baton Rouge. They couldn't.

As I lie in the truck in the shattered city, something else bothers me. On no previous story had I been unable to find words to describe the immensity of a tragedy. In a profession for which overstatement is a bylaw, it's impossible to exaggerate Katrina.

For the past week, I've been thinking about a quote I encountered several years ago while doing research on the Great Galveston Storm of 1900, which killed some 6,000 people and destroyed that graceful coastal city. Now I finally understand it. An old woman who survived the terrible hurricane as a young girl had put it this way, "Aw, it was an awful thing. You want me to tell you, but no tongue can tell it."